THE CANADA GOOSE

Kit Howard Breen

VOYAGEUR PRESS

Dedicated to the many individuals and to the organizations,
both public and private, helping preserve and protect the Canada Goose and its habitat

Copyright © 1990 by Kit Howard Breen

Printed in Hong Kong

90 91 92 93 94   5 4 3 2 1

Library of Congress Cataloging-in-Publication Data

Breen, Kit Howard.
    The Canada goose / Kit Howard Breen.
        p.   cm.
    Includes bibliographical references.
    ISBN 0-89658-121-7
    1. Canada goose. 2. Wildlife conservation. I. Title.
QL696.A52B73   1990
598.4'1—dc20   89-70600
                                                     CIP

Published by Voyageur Press, Inc.
P.O. Box 338
123 North Second Street
Stillwater, MN 55082 U.S.A.
In Minn 612-430-2210
Toll-free 800-888-9653

Voyageur Press books are also available at discounts for bulk quantities for educational, fundraising, premium, or sales-promotion use. For details contact the marketing manager. Please write or call for our free catalog of natural history publications.

CONTENTS

INTRODUCTION

Of all the species of birds in the world, none has such a large and enthusiastic following as the Canada Goose. People from all walks of life share a common bond in their affection for Canada Geese. All along the migratory flyways, people rush to their windows or pause from their outdoor chores when the first honks are heard overhead as each fall the flocks fly south toward their winter homes. Even people who usually pay little attention to birds look with anticipation for the return of the geese. They are eager to greet the new arrivals as the warm days of Indian summer turn fields and meadows to gold and as crisp nights bring fog to the marshes and sloughs. Few species inspire such passionate loyalty from so many people.

It is little wonder that Canada Geese are so popular. They are magnificent in flight as they carve through the skies in great undulating V-shaped formations. On land they have a stately appearance, walking with more grace and ease than other species of waterfowl.

Initially, we are drawn to the spectacle of the wild geese. Their strangeness, their ability to do what we cannot do and long to do—fly—engages us. Then our bond with them strengthens when we discover in Canada Geese characteristics and ideals that we identify as human. Canada Geese do not believe in divorce; they mate for life. So strong is the pair bond between them that if one is wounded and unable to fly, the mate will abandon the flock to stay with the wounded partner no matter what danger that may pose. When the rest of the flock migrates in the spring, the pair with one wounded bird remain together, perhaps raising a family where they have wintered over. Canada Geese are also superb parents. They closely guard their goslings, fiercely defending them against predators, until the young geese are fully capable of defending themselves.

The late Sir Peter Scott was a British painter whose lovely oil paintings and drawings of waterfowl are much prized by enthusiasts in Europe. A dedicated conservationist and naturalist, he founded the Wildfowl Trust, a nonprofit organization that maintains seven waterfowl refuges in England. Sir Peter, the first person knighted in England for services on behalf of conservation of the environment, wrote of his love affair with geese in his book *Observations of Wildlife*:

The Wild Geese had captured my imagination, and if the two words are printed with capital letters, this is merely to indicate that they had become, and have remained, a kind of obsession. Wild Geese . . . are very special birds because their society is based on a permanent pair bond and a family life which keeps the young with their parents until breeding times comes around again. . . . As birds go, they are rather intelligent. They make long and still incompletely understood migrations, they fly in skeins at dawn and dusk, calling most tunefully, and often they

4

gather in vast aggregations which constitute, in many countries, the finest wildlife spectacle still to be seen. All of these things give the Wild Geese . . . a special magic in the hearts and minds of most people who have come to know them well over a long period of time. It is more than 50 years since I first fell under their spell, and I remain totally addicted to their magic. So when I went to learn to paint, it was largely to be able to paint my Wild Geese better.

Other naturalists have shared Sir Peter Scott's love for the geese. Frank Bellrose, eminent waterfowl biologist and author of the classic work on waterfowl management *Ducks, Geese and Swans of North America*, has been studying waterfowl since 1935. In an article about Bellrose written by Mike Rotide for *National Wildlife*, the author describes Frank's lifetime dedication to duck research, calling him "the undisputed dean of duck researchers." In an interview for this article, Rotide asked Bellrose, "After all the years of slogging through the marshes and writing up observations, is there anything in life that excites you as much as ducks do?" Bellrose replied smiling, "Oh indeed yes. GEESE!"

James Michener, in his epic novel *Chesapeake*, draws a most affectionate portrait of the Canada Goose. A gander named Onk-or and his family are the protagonists in the chapter titled "Voyage Eight: 1822." They are pitted against Lafe Turlock and his sons, owners of the Choptank River farm and marshes where Onk-or and his

family spend the winter. Michener beautifully captures the spirit of Maryland's Eastern Shore residents and their passion for Canada Geese. According to Lafe Turlock, "The life of man is divided into two seasons. 'Geese is here. Geese ain't here.' "

Michener's description of his goose characters is more eloquent than those found in the birding guides and encyclopedias. Onk-or and "his mate were handsome birds, large and sleek. Both they and their children had long necks feathered in jet-black, with a broad snowy white bib under the chin and reaching to the ears. When their wings were folded, as they were most of the time, the heavy body was compact and beautifully proportioned, and they walked with dignity, not waddling from side to side like ducks. Their heads were finely proportioned, with bills pointed but not grotesquely long, and the lines of their bodies, where feathers of differing shades of gray joined, were pleasing."

For many people, geese are not just an interest, a hobby, or a passing fancy, but rather a *serious* passion—and I number among those people. My discussion of the Canada Goose is divided into four major sections, each corresponding to one of the four seasons. Since my experiences with geese are limited to observing and photographing them, I have borrowed significantly from other writers so that this book might present an overview of our knowledge of and appreciation for Canada Geese.

"Canada Goose with Grasses."

FALL: TRAVELERS RETURN TO WINTER HOMES

They come from Alaska, they come from Newfoundland and Labrador, they come from the arctic tundra near James and Hudson bays, from northern Alberta and Saskatchewan, these majestic Canada Geese filling the early October skies with their excitement. They come by the hundreds of thousands in great flocks, the young with their parents, grandparents, aunts, uncles, and cousins, traveling together in large extended families to the same wintering grounds year after year. Where they nest and the routes they travel southward for the winter are well mapped. The various subspecies of Canada Geese have their specific territories for nesting and for wintering. When they travel, how far they migrate, and where they rest along the routes are predictable from previous years' data. But how they navigate, finding their way year after year to the same place, remains a mystery.

MIGRATION FLYWAYS AND CORRIDORS

The migrating geese travel down long-established routes covering much of Canada, Alaska, and the United States. Wildlife biologists have tracked these routes and classified them several ways. The simplest classification has divided the waterfowl migration routes into four major flyways: Atlantic, Pacific, Mississippi, and Central. These four flyways encompass broad north-to-south routes over major river valleys and coastal wetlands.

Recent research has suggested that the flyway classification is an oversimplification. Bellrose (1976) proposed instead dividing the waterfowl migration routes into "migration corridors," literally duck and goose highways in the air. Bellrose has spent years researching the migration routes of various species of ducks, geese, and swans. Using radar tracking reports for waterfowl, ground observations, and data from airplane pilots reporting the location and direction of flights, Bellrose mapped the migration corridors for Canada Geese. Each goose migration corridor is a strip approximately thirty to fifty miles wide that follows the course of river valleys, or lakes and coastal marshes, so that the birds have safe resting areas, food, and water along the way. Canada Geese prefer sleeping on the water; this is apparently much safer than sleeping on land where foxes and other predators could easily attack them at night.

As the map "Goose Migration Corridors" (on page 9) illustrates, much of the North American continent is crossed by migrating geese. The middle sections of Canada and the United States have the broadest coverage for goose migrations as the birds follow the prairie potholes, river valleys, and lakes south toward warmer climates for the winter. A large number of geese nest in central Canada around Hudson Bay, up into the arctic tundra, and in the lake country of Manitoba, Ontario, and Quebec provinces. One migration corridor for these central Canadian nesters

"Flight at Dusk." (Photo by Jan Lucie)

"Resting on the Refuge."

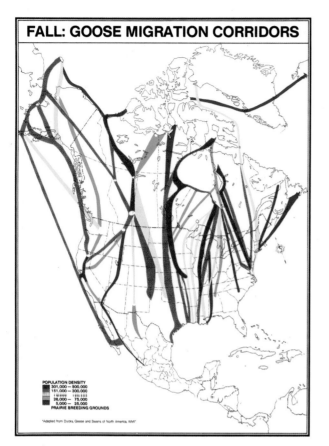

FALL: GOOSE MIGRATION CORRIDORS

POPULATION DENSITY
301,000 — 500,000
151,000 — 300,000
76,000 — 150,000
26,000 — 75,000
5,000 — 25,000
PRAIRIE BREEDING GROUNDS

Adapted from Ducks, Geese and Swans of North America, WMI

Populations in goose migration corridors. Source: Frank Bellrose (1987) in David Wesley and William Leitch's Fireside Waterfowler. *Reproduced with the kind permission of Stackpole Books and Ducks Unlimited.*

generally follows a straight line south from the lower Hudson Bay region across Lake Superior down through Wisconsin to southern Illinois, where the numbers of geese have been increasing. Horicon National Wildlife Refuge in eastern Wisconsin has as many as 500,000 geese resting there during the fall migration, which indicates that in recent years these numbers have somewhat increased. Another group of geese from central Canada take a more westerly route down through Manitoba, Minnesota, western Iowa, and eastern Kansas to the Texas coast.

Large numbers of Canada Geese nest around Hudson Bay and throughout much of eastern Canada. These birds follow a migration corridor that crosses Quebec province, then drops down through western New York and central Pennsylvania to the Delmarva Peninsula, which lies between Chesapeake and Delaware bays and comprises Delaware and parts of Maryland and

Virginia. These are the famous geese of Maryland's Eastern Shore, the "Goose Hunting Capital of the World."

GOOSE POPULATIONS

Waterfowl management biologists classify Canada Geese by "populations" for the purpose of counting them and keeping track of the rise and fall of their numbers in different parts of the United States and Canada. The division into twelve separate populations is based on the nesting area, migration route, and wintering grounds of each group. Cadieux (1986) lists the twelve populations of migrating geese, and describes the territory some populations inhabit, as well as the subspecies that make up these populations.

Populations of Migrating Geese
 1. North Atlantic Population
 2. Mid-Atlantic Population
 3. Tennessee Valley Population
 4. Mississippi Valley Population
 5. Eastern Prairie Population
 6. Western Prairie Population
 7. Tall Grass Prairie Population
 8. Short Grass Prairie Population
 9. Highline Population
10. Intermountain Population
11. Northwest Coastal Population
12. Alaskan Population

The North Atlantic Population are geese that nest in Newfoundland and Labrador and migrate along the coast to their wintering grounds in New England and the mid-Atlantic states down to North Carolina. This fairly small population of geese is made up of just one subspecies of Canada Goose, *Branta canadensis canadensis*. According to Cadieux, the Atlantic population used to winter all the way south to the Gulf coast. Apparently, milder winters plus the ready availability of corn, one of their favorite foods, near the coastal areas of Maryland and Delaware are partially responsible for changes in the winter habits of this population. It is also likely that hunting pressure and heavy harvest rates were important factors in reducing the size of the more southern

Canada Geese dropping into a cornfield.

"Four Geese Reflected."

wintering flocks.

A much larger group of wintering geese comprise the Mid-Atlantic Population. Bellrose (1976) describes this population as composed primarily of the subspecies *Branta canadensis interior*, with a small number of the Giant Canada Geese, *Branta canadensis maxima*. The Interior subspecies nests from the Ungava Peninsula in northern Quebec province across the Hudson Bay and James Bay wetlands, and up into the tundra areas of central Canada. Most of these birds travel a considerable distance to winter on the Delmarva Peninsula where they mix with the North Atlantic Population.

The Mississippi Valley Population and the Tennessee Valley Population consist primarily of the Interior subspecies of Canada Geese plus Giant Canadas, according to Bellrose (1976). Moving farther west, the composition of the populations changes. The Eastern Prairie Population winters from Minnesota, Iowa, and Missouri south to Arkansas and western Louisiana. It consists primarily of the Interior race, several thousand of the smaller races, and a sizable proportion of the Giant race. The Western Prairie Population, mostly the Interior race with a few Giants and some smaller western races, breeds in northwestern Manitoba and northern Saskatchewan. They migrate down the Missouri River Valley to Lake Andes and the Fort Randall Reservoir in South Dakota, and to Squaw Creek in Missouri where the majority of this population winter. A few birds from this population straggle down to the Red River in Texas. The Short Grass Prairie Population has very few of the Interior strain, consisting instead almost entirely of the Lesser Canada Goose, *Branta canadensis parvipes*. The Highline Population consists of geese that breed in the high plains regions and on ponds and reservoirs just east of the Rocky Mountains from Saskatchewan and Alberta south through central Montana and Wyoming to Colorado. These are primarily the Western or Great Basin race plus some Giant Canada Geese. They migrate a short distance to Eastern Colorado and to Bosque del Apache Refuge in New Mexico for the winter. The Northwest Coastal Population consists primarily of two different subspecies of Canada Geese, the beautiful Dusky Canada, *Branta canadensis occidentalis*, as well as the Vancouver Canada, *Branta canadensis fulva*. The Dusky Canadas nest in coastal Alaska and migrate to winter homes in Oregon. Small numbers of the Western Goose, *Branta canadensis moffitti*, and the Cackling Canada Goose, *Branta canadensis minima*, are also mixed in the Northwest Coastal Population.

SUBSPECIES OR RACES

As evident from the discussion of populations, not all Canada Geese are alike. Many goose watchers are completely unaware of the wide variety of Canada Geese since they commonly see only one wintering subspecies in their location. Some distinctions between the subspecies are subtle so that only the experienced biologist can tell one subspecies from another. A few of the subspecies or races, however, are very distinctive, especially the Dusky, the Cackling, and the Giant Canada races.

Waterfowl biologists disagree considerably about how many races of Canada Geese should be recognized. Palmer (1976) lists eight subspecies; Todd (1979) mentions twelve subspecies; Bellrose (1976) lists eleven subspecies of Canada Geese.

Subspecies of Canada Geese
1. *Branta canadensis canadensis*, Atlantic Canada Goose
2. *Branta canadensis interior*, Hudson Bay Canada Goose
3. *Branta canadensis maxima*, Giant Canada Goose
4. *Branta canadensis moffitti*, Great Basin Canada Goose
5. *Branta canadensis parvipes*, Lesser Canada Goose
6. *Branta canadensis taverneri*, Alaskan Canada Goose
7. *Branta canadensis fulva*, Vancouver Canada Goose
8. *Branta canadensis occidentalis*, Dusky Canada Goose
9. *Branta canadensis leucopareia*, Aleutian Canada Goose

10. *Branta canadensis minima*, Cackling Canada Goose
11. *Branta canadensis hutchinsii*, Richardson Canada Goose

The classification into different races is based on the range of the geese, their size, the shape of their heads and necks, feather coloration, overall proportions, and distinctive voice and calls. Each subspecies, for example, has different calls and a distinctive pitch; generally the larger the subspecies, the deeper the voice. In size, the subspecies of Canada Geese range from the small three- to four-pound Cackling Goose to the nine- to fourteen-pound Giant Canada Goose. The Richardson and the Aleutian races, both western dwellers, are very small birds, weighing around three pounds. The smaller races tend to breed farther north and to the west. And the smaller, more western Canada Geese also have darker rather than pale gray or creamy breasts. The *occidentalis* or Dusky Canada Goose is particularly striking with its coffee coloring below and dark brown to black feathers on back and wings. The small Cackling Goose has a shorter neck and slightly different head from the other races of Canada Geese. The larger geese have paler breasts and look much alike except for size.

Some field guides to birds do mention different subspecies of Canada Geese. Roger Tory Peterson's *Field Guide of Western Birds* (1941) gives descriptions of five subspecies of Canadas, and a drawing illustrates the relative sizes of the Cackling, Lesser, and Common or Atlantic Canada Geese. A better depiction of five subspecies is given in the National Geographic Society's *Field Guide to Birds of North America* (1983). In that guide detailed drawings show the coloring and different head and neck shapes, as well as the relative sizes of the Cackling, Aleutian, Richardson, Dusky, and Atlantic Canada Geese.

Frank Todd (1979) describes many of the subspecies of Canada Geese in *Waterfowl: Ducks, Geese, and Swans of the World*, and the following descriptions of the different races rely on his work.

The Atlantic Canada Goose (*B. c. canadensis*) is also known as the Common Canada Goose. This race has a creamy light upper breast with slightly less white underparts. They have substantial bodies and long graceful necks. These are thought to be the race of geese introduced from North America into Great Britain in 1670, and much later into New Zealand and Scandinavia. The population of the Atlantic Canada Geese in England in 1976 was nearly 20,000.

Moffitt's Canada Goose (*B. c. moffitti*), also referred to as the Western or Great Basin Canada Goose, is sometimes bigger than the Atlantic race, but at the same time sleeker in the body. It is usually a little darker in its underparts and has a long thin neck.

The Interior or Hudson Bay Canada Goose (*B. c. interior*) is very much like the Atlantic Canada Goose, but perhaps a little smaller and less creamy below. Moving farther west, the Lesser Canada Goose (*B. c. parvipes*) is quite a bit smaller than the Atlantic Canada Goose.

In the far West, both the Dusky Canada Goose (*B. c. occidentalis*) and the Vancouver Canada Goose (*B. c. fulva*) are considerably darker in their lower feathering than the eastern races. These two races are fairly large, weighing eight or nine pounds for the Dusky, and ten to thirteen pounds for the nonmigrating Vancouver race.

Two of the Alaskan breeding races, the Alaskan or Taverner's Goose and the Cackling Canada Goose, are the smallest in size of all the races. The Alaskan Canada (*B. c. taverneri*) weighs four to five pounds. Its bill and neck are shorter than many races, and it may have a slight narrow white neck ring. The tiny Cackling Goose (*B. c. minima*) has a distinctly shorter neck and smaller head and weighs only three to four pounds. Cackling Geese also have dark feathers below similar to those of the Dusky Goose. In addition to their unique proportions, Cackling Geese have a very different voice from those of the other races, and their distinctive, high-pitched incessant chatter earned them their common name.

Three subspecies that are not described by Todd are the Richardson Canada Goose (*Branta canadensis hutchinsii*), the Aleutian Canada Goose (*Branta canadensis leucopareia*), and the Giant

A Cackling Canada Goose.

Canada Goose (*Branta canadensis maxima*). Palmer (1976) and others offer us details about these races. The Richardson Goose is thought to be descended from the same lineage as the Atlantic Canada Goose. It has a pale underbody similar to that of the Atlantic race, but is much smaller in size, only a little larger than the Cackling Goose. The bill is more stubby and the neck shorter than that of the larger Atlantic Goose.

The Aleutian Canada Goose is a small goose, as are all the Alaskan geese, with dark underparts, the upper breast often being quite dark near the sharply defined white collar present in some but not all of this race. The head of this endangered race is squarish and its legs long.

The Giant Canada Goose, once thought to be extinct, is the largest of the races, and the most elongated in shape. It has pale underparts. Often it has a white mark on the head above the bill, and sometimes the white chin strap extends farther up the side of the head than it does for other races. Some Giant Canada Geese have white collars at the bottom of the black neck. The Giant is considerably larger in size and weight than the more common varieties of Canadas. Giant Canada Geese usually weigh nine to fourteen pounds, but individuals of this race have been reported weighing as much as twenty-two pounds.

RECOVERING SUBSPECIES

Some subspecies have come near to extinction. The Giant Canada Goose was apparently common across much of the Great Plains and the Mississippi Flyway when the United States was first settled by Europeans. The great bird was heavily hunted, an easy target because of its large size. Giant Canadas were also raised early in the twentieth century as living decoys that were highly effective in attracting flying birds. When the use of live decoys was outlawed in 1935, the number of Giants began to decline until only a few were left in small captive flocks. Through conservation efforts on the part of several individuals and organizations, the Giant Canada today numbers close to 200,000.

13

A subspecies that remains close to extinction is the Aleutian Goose, which nests on a few small islands in the Aleutian chain. The Aleutian Goose almost disappeared when residents of these islands began raising arctic foxes for skins. The foxes prospered in part because of the Aleutian Geese which they obviously found delectable. By 1962 the only remaining Aleutian Geese were on the island of Buldir where no foxes had been introduced. The U.S. Fish and Wildlife Service captured several of the Buldir Island geese and took them to Patuxent, Maryland for breeding. After several years of breeding, some captive birds were reintroduced to the Aleutian Islands. In order to accomplish the restocking, the foxes, which were not native to the Aleutians, were removed from several of the islands. While these geese are still endangered, they do seem to be increasing in number thanks to conservation efforts.

The Dusky Canada has been declining in numbers in recent years due to changes in its nesting habitat in the Copper River Delta of Alaska. Apparently the 1973 earthquake in that region changed the habitat considerably, reducing the areas suitable for nesting. In addition, the growth of brushy cover followed changes from the earthquake, making the region more attractive to grizzly bears. The increased number of bears in the nesting area has cut goose production since the bears appear to like goose omelets for lunch! The disastrous Exxon oil spill near the port of Valdez in the spring of 1989 may well affect the production of the Dusky Canada Goose since some of that race nests in the Prince William Sound area.

While certain subspecies have been declining in numbers, others are holding their own or growing in numbers. According to the U.S. Fish and Wildlife Service, data from its annual mid-winter counts of all geese show an increase in total goose numbers over the long term. However, while the total numbers of geese are growing, the distribution of these numbers remains a problem in many areas.

A Giant Canada Goose.

LONG AND SHORT MIGRATIONS OF DIFFERENT RACES

The migration of Canada Geese varies in different races from over a thousand miles for geese that nest in the northern reaches of Canada to a few hundred miles for some races nesting in Alaska. Most of the Vancouver race does not migrate at all, spending both winter and summer in British Columbia. Climate and food supply seem to be two main factors influencing how far Canada Geese migrate. When the winters stay warmer, geese may not migrate as far south as they do when the winters are especially cold. Open water for resting and drinking and food that is not frozen solid seem to be two major requirements for geese.

The pattern of migration and the numbers of wintering geese have changed radically over the past several decades. On the one hand, the total population of Canada Geese wintering in the United States doubled between 1955 and 1974, according to Bellrose (1976). The increase was due largely to good wildlife management practices by state and federal authorities. On the other hand, some states experienced a decline in the numbers of wintering Canada Geese. California, Texas, Oklahoma, Mississippi, and Louisiana, for example, have fewer geese than they had years ago. North and South Carolina have also experienced drastic declines in their wintering goose population since 1969. In the past three years, Maryland and Delaware have seen significant declines in their numbers of geese, much to the consternation of hunters.

Almost all of Canada and most of the United States except for Mississippi, Alabama, Georgia, and Florida have one or another of the races of Canada Geese either migrating through to and from the nesting areas or wintering over. Bellrose supplies a pair of maps, one for the smaller darker races of the Canada Goose (Dusky, Cackling, Lesser, Alaskan, and Aleutian), the other for the medium and larger races. These two maps (on pages 16 and 17) reveal that the smaller, darker races are found west of the Mississippi River,

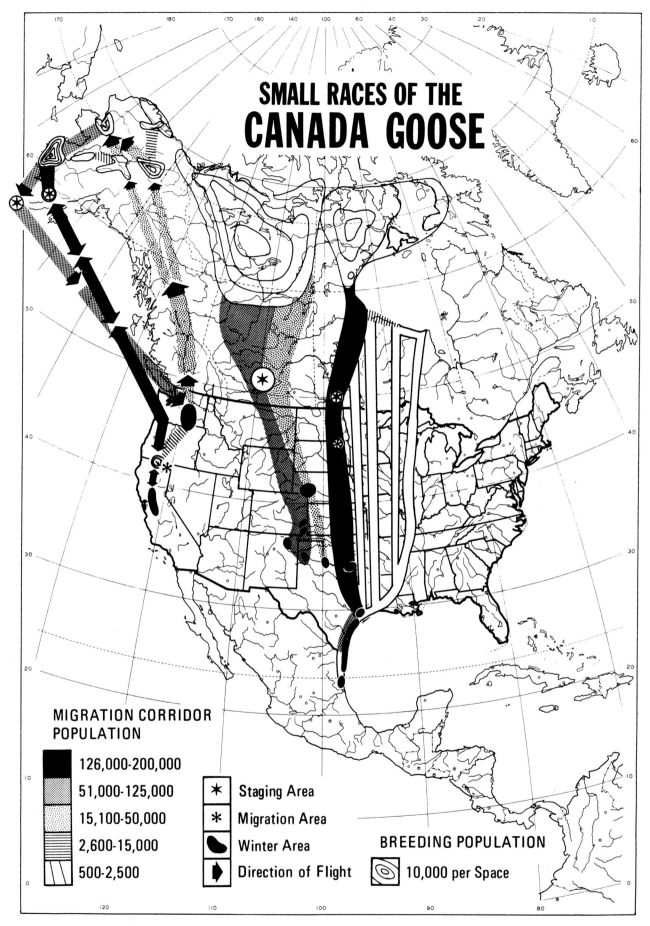

SMALL RACES OF THE CANADA GOOSE

MIGRATION CORRIDOR POPULATION

- 126,000-200,000
- 51,000-125,000
- 15,100-50,000
- 2,600-15,000
- 500-2,500

✳ Staging Area

✱ Migration Area

⬛ Winter Area

➤ Direction of Flight

BREEDING POPULATION

◎ 10,000 per Space

Migration corridors for the smaller races of Canada Geese. Source: Frank Bellrose (1976) Ducks, Geese and Swans of North America. *Reproduced with the kind permission of Stackpole Books and the Wildlife Management Institute.*

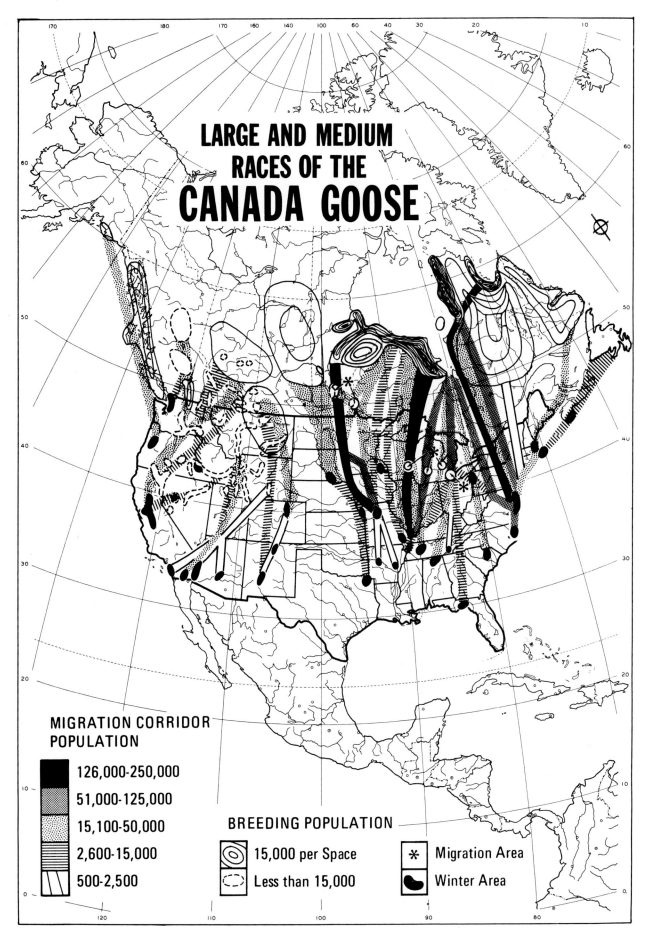

LARGE AND MEDIUM RACES OF THE CANADA GOOSE

MIGRATION CORRIDOR POPULATION

126,000-250,000
51,000-125,000
15,100-50,000
2,600-15,000
500-2,500

BREEDING POPULATION

15,000 per Space
Less than 15,000

* Migration Area
Winter Area

Migration corridors for the medium and large races of Canada Geese. Source: Frank Bellrose (1976) Duck, Geese and Swans of North America. *Reproduced with the kind permission of Stackpole Books and the Wildlife Management Institute.*

"Geese in the Marsh."

while the large-and medium-sized birds gather east of the Mississippi River. Note the black patches on the maps which indicate major winter concentrations of Canada Geese.

HOW GEESE NAVIGATE

How birds find their way to migrate thousands of miles from one specific nesting ground to another specific wintering home presents one of the great mysteries of the natural world. It is truly remarkable that flocks of birds find their course in good weather and in bad, by day and by night, to the exact location of their summer nesting grounds and their winter havens year after year. Scientists have studied a variety of data in their attempts to understand how birds navigate. The information used to develop an understanding of bird navigation includes bird banding, radar tracking, reports from hunters and other observers, and laboratory and field experiments.

Much more is known about when and where geese migrate than is known about how they navigate. From experimental work done with other birds, it seems probable that geese like other species use several different cues to plot their course from summer to winter homes and back again. Several theories seek to explain bird navigation; each is supported by various types of data.

Banding is one of the major methods used to track the flight of birds. The birds, including Canada Geese, are caught in the wild with thin nets, banded with tiny numbered aluminum rings attached to one leg, and then immediately released. The date and location of the banding is then recorded and the data sent to the U.S. Fish and Wildlife Service. Anyone capturing or shooting a banded bird should report the date, location, and condition of the bird recovered to the Bird Banding Laboratory of the U.S. Fish and Wildlife Service, Department of the Interior, in Laurel, Maryland. It maintains records of every bird that is banded in the United States and Canada. From reports sent in by people who re-

"Into the Sunset."

cover banded birds, much is learned about the birds' travels, their longevity, the reasons for their death, and their general health. Banding is one main source of data that proves waterfowl return to the same nesting and wintering locations year after year.

Another type of band, the large neck collar, is sometimes used for studies of geese and swans. The collars are usually yellow with large black numbers that can be read at a distance with field glasses or at close range with good eyesight. With these neck collars, the birds can be easily identified and reported without having to recapture or kill them.

Radar tracking of flocks of birds has produced data about the speed of flight, altitudes, and approximate numbers of birds following a particular flight path. Data reported from airline pilots observing the direction of migrating flocks, plus information from radar tracking, has greatly added to our knowledge of the migration routes, the speed of flight, and the timing of the journeys

made by different species. For example, it has been established that songbirds migrate primarily at night, presumably to reduce the hazards from predators. Waterfowl, on the other hand, fly both day and night on their migratory journeys.

Bellrose has studied waterfowl migration extensively. From his research he concluded that geese like other species of birds use many different cues for navigation. The cues used by different species of ducks and geese have all evolved according to the specific needs of the species and the distances and conditions under which each migrates. Since waterfowl need bodies of water for resting at night and for feeding, they must be able to navigate between lakes and rivers on their way north and south. Because of their need to find suitable water bodies on their flight path, ducks and geese need more precise navigation than most species of songbirds. Bellrose believes that geese rely heavily on landscape cues to guide them. He has watched hundreds of flocks suddenly change the direction of their flight by 35 to 45 degrees, apparently in response to a landmark the birds recognize. On clear nights, geese follow the contours of bodies of water in their migrating flights. When there is thick cloud cover at night, some flocks overshoot their home wintering grounds, necessitating a reversal of course the following day when visibility is better.

But landscape cues are not the sole method used by waterfowl for guidance. Many geese and ducks fly over large landmasses without distinguishing features and yet arrive exactly at their destinations. Field observations of migrating geese suggest they use the positions of the sun and the stars as navigational aids. Geese have very keen eyesight which probably helps them to see their own constellations or patterns in the stars. Birds appear to use the north star to find their direction at night. Evidence to support this theory comes from experiments in which birds were placed indoors in rooms with lights simulating the constellations. As the simulated night sky is rotated, the birds change their direction of movement to follow the correct migration course north or south. While none of these experiments have been done using waterfowl as subjects, Bellrose and other waterfowl biologists infer from field data that geese and ducks use the stars for guidance when the landscape below is invisible.

Radar data has shown that geese and ducks occasionally migrate when the cloud cover is dense or when a fog blankets the landscape—and yet the birds still find their way. The flight pattern may be more dispersed under conditions of low visibility, but the direction of the flight is still right on target. From this radar data, it is evident that waterfowl may use some cues for direction finding other than landscape features and the positions of the sun and stars. Bellrose believes that waterfowl can use the earth's magnetic field to find their course when the more obvious cues from the landscape and the sun or stars are obscured.

Experiments conducted in the field with homing pigeons and gulls support the theory that birds have built-in compasses that respond to the earth's magnetic field. Scientists have found iron-rich tissue in the brains of some birds; presumably it responds much as a compass does. To test whether or not birds are affected by magnetic disturbances, homing pigeons were released near a large magnetic iron deposit in Rhode Island. The homing pigeons were unable to find their way home when they were released near the huge iron deposit, which created a strong local magnetic field different from the earth's. The farther away from the magnetic field of the iron deposit, the better the pigeons were able to reorient themselves to fly home. According to Bellrose, recent field experiments that have used ducks and geese as subjects have indicated that waterfowl are capable of using the earth's magnetic field to guide them. He believes that waterfowl have some type of built-in compass similar to the iron tissue in the heads of pigeons.

FLIGHT BEHAVIOR

Canada Geese are graceful and smooth in their flight, appearing to glide through the air with ease and assurance. They often fly in loose, ever-changing V-shaped formations, close to one another so that they may take advantage of the slipstream effect from the bird ahead. Flying in a V formation greatly reduces air resistance for the birds, allowing them to fly 71 percent further in a formation than they could fly by themselves, according to Terres (1980). By positioning itself slightly to one side and behind the bird ahead, a goose gets lift from the air currents coming off the wing tips of the bird ahead. The rising air current from the bird in front saves energy on the lift-up phase of the wing beat. Since all birds except the hummingbird have very strong muscles for the down beat, but much weaker muscles for the up beat, the borrowed lift from the bird ahead helps the up-beat stroke. This enables birds to fly longer and farther than they could without the added up current.

It is thought that the dominant gander of the flock leads the migration flight south in the fall. Some believe that the leading goose changes from time to time (Terres 1980). On the spring migration, there is evidence that the dominant

Flying in a V formation reduces air resistance.

V-shaped flight formations are fluid, constantly changing in shape.

21

"Look Out Below!"

When the weather is windy, Canada Geese may whiffle.

gander's mate leads the flock on the final leg of the flight to the nesting site. On local flights at the wintering grounds, frequently the dominant gander announces to the flock that it is time to take off by a vigorous tossing of his head accompanied by soft sounds. The female may lead the local flight with the gander bringing up the rear.

Unless the flock is startled so that all the geese explode into the air at once, there is an obvious change in behavior several minutes before takeoff. One or more geese may begin a loud persistent honking, as they turn their faces into the wind. If they are on land, they may begin to walk in the direction of takeoff—always into the wind—while on the water they swim into the wind. In big flocks, family units may take off one at a time rather than the whole large group leaving at once.

During migration, Canada Geese travel in flocks consisting of extended family units. The majority of flocks fly at altitudes between 1,000 and 3,000 feet, although they can easily fly over

mountain ranges 12,000 feet high. In poor weather with low visibility, geese may fly as low as several hundred feet off the ground. They fly by day or night in any kind of weather. They appear to use favorable wind currents, sometimes arriving at their winter quarters with a tail wind to help them along (Bellrose 1976).

Canada Geese fly at speeds of forty-two to forty-five miles per hour, much slower than many species of ducks. A red-breasted merganser, for example, was clocked by an airplane at eighty miles per hour, and a male canvasback at seventy-two. Canvasbacks, pintails, and other speedy flying ducks appear to have an almost frantic flight compared to the much more relaxed flight of geese.

While taking off seems very graceful and easy for Canada Geese, landing can be a little awkward. They come in for a landing on ground or water with their feet stretched out forward and their toes spread wide. Their necks are often bent downward so they can see where they land.

Whiffling Canada Geese.

"Comical Whifflers."

Geese may look rather comical as they settle down to land.

Landing in a strong wind is even more difficult for these large birds. Apparently it is not good etiquette to land on top of your neighbor, so extra care must be taken to avoid such embarrassment when it is windy. At least, that is one theory about the strange landing behavior geese and some ducks exhibit on windy days. Many people have never seen the acrobatic whiffling, or mapleleafing, of geese landing in a high wind. When a flock is gliding in to land, at about 100 feet above the ground, some geese begin to whiffle. They turn on their sides, spilling the wind from their outstretched wings, causing them to drop precipitously five or ten feet at a time, before spreading their wings to right themselves. Sometimes they turn over completely in a 360-degree roll in the air. More often they turn sideways 180 degrees onto their backs and then back again to upright.

Just why geese and ducks whiffle no one knows for sure. Only a few geese in the flock whiffle when landing. Some experienced hunting guides have told me that mostly the young geese exhibit this behavior. If that is so, they may simply be showing off and having a good time. It may also be that the younger geese, being less practiced at flying, may be unsure how to land where they wish in heavy wind. They may use the rapid decent to help them pinpoint their landing. The older geese may know better how to judge where they will land with a long glide on windy days. Whatever the reason, the behavior is certainly amusing to watch, not to mention a real challenge to photograph!

GOOSE AIR EXPRESS

Some of the most incredible stories I've come across concerning the Canada Goose suggest that geese occasionally become passenger planes for very small birds, carrying them tucked into their feathers during migration flights. Both reports from individual observers and from folk-

lore of several Indian tribes tell of geese, cranes, and other large migratory birds carrying tiny birds on their backs. These reports come from various parts of the world from people having no connection with one another who, therefore, could not have influenced each other in the telling of these tales. John K. Terres (1987), a well-respected naturalist and author of *The Audubon Society Encyclopedia of North American Birds*, in an article for *National Wildlife*, discusses a number of published reports about hitchhiking birds.

Terres was intrigued by the story of a goose shot in British Columbia that appeared to be carrying a small hummingbird in its feathers. He remembered that his grandmother had repeated a tale she heard from a bay fisherman living along the New Jersey marshes who said he had shot a goose or swan that was carrying a small songbird. Terres began searching for more published reports of these phenomena and came across a number of references to such happenings, many of them concerning Canada Geese. One story occurs in a book by Al Martin who retired to a cabin in Maine a few years ago. A visiting friend presented Martin with a goose shot that morning. After laying the goose on the table, the friend then removed from his tobacco pouch a male hummingbird, saying that the tiny bird was still breathing when he first picked up the goose, but died in his hands. It is interesting that in both this tale from Maine and the story from British Columbia hummingbirds act as passengers.

Terres uncovered other similar tales in his research. A hunter on the coast of England claimed to have shot a goose with a small hitchhiker. An English sea captain reported that, while in the Mediterranean Sea, he had observed a flock of geese migrating north. With his telescope, the captain saw tiny birds rise from the backs of the geese and then return to them.

Two North American Indian tribes were reported in the last century to have told tales of small birds riding the backs of Canada Geese. John Rae, a Scotsman who explored the northern portion of Canada in the late nineteenth century, wrote in 1878 that the Cree Indians living along Hudson Bay told of sparrows and finches hitching rides on the backs of migrating Canada Geese. In the same year, another naturalist, a U.S. Army doctor stationed in Montana, wrote about the Crow Indians' description of sandhill and whooping cranes carrying small birds on their migration flights.

Certainly no scientific documentation supports these tales. Apparently no well-known ornithologists have made such observations. However, with such a wide number of stories surfacing from so many independent sources around the world, it seems more than likely that this is indeed a genuine behavior that occurs not frequently, but from time to time, with Canada Geese and other large migrating birds. "Goose air express leaving in twenty minutes. All passengers choose your goose and climb aboard. Destinations north."

An interesting question, given that small birds actually do hitch rides, is: Are the geese and cranes willing expresses for their small passengers? Most likely, the larger birds both know the small ones are riding and accept it. It should not be very difficult for a goose to dump a would-be passenger if he or she did not care to act as carrier. Geese can twist and roll in the air, even turn upside down in the air if they wish, as they often demonstrate when whiffling on windy days. On the ground they could certainly dislodge unwanted hitchhikers by fluffing their feathers and flapping their wings as they do when bathing. So why do geese and cranes allow passengers on their long flights? — An intriguing question to which we shall probably never have an answer.

"All Passengers, Board Your Goose! Air Express Leaving Now."

WINTER: GAME BIRDS

A few Canada Geese stay year-round among people who live south of the arctic tundra, the traditional nesting grounds for most geese. But the majority of people on the North American continent see Canada Geese only for a portion of the year when they pass overhead on their migratory flights, or as winter sojourners basking in the warmer climates and more plentiful food supplies of the temperate zone. During the late fall and winter, the geese become for some people the most prized of game birds.

People have long been harvesters of waterfowl. Indians and Inuit harvested ducks and geese before Europeans arrived. The vast North American continent seemed to provide a limitless abundance of many species of ducks and geese—more than enough for all who wished to take them. And so the settlers moving west hunted the birds first for food, then later for sport. The plains states were favorite hunting grounds, attracting hunters from many nearby cities and towns. Only more recently have hunters, like others who cannot live without wild things, become stewards of waterfowl, and realized that a sports hunting ethic and game management must be a part of their passion for ducks and geese.

Aldo Leopold, an American naturalist who is often called the father of game management, helped awake concern for conservation by putting the right questions to people, as he does in his essay "Goose Music."

"Goose Music."

. . . I have congenital hunting fever and three sons. As little tots, they spent their time playing with my decoys and scouring vacant lots with wooden guns. I hope to leave them good health, an education, and possibly even a competence. But what are they going to do with these things if there be no more deer in the hills, and no more quail in the coverts? No more snipe whisting in the meadow, no more piping of widgeons and chattering of teal as darkness covers the marshes; no more whisting of swift wings when the morning star pales in the east? And when the dawn-wind stirs through the ancient cottonwoods, and the gray light steals down from the hills over the old river sliding softly past its wide brown sandbars—what if there be no more goose music?

GOOSE HUNTERS, FROM PICKUP TRUCKS TO JETS

Goose hunting attracts a wide range of people from all walks of life. They congregate by the thousands in goose hunting meccas such as Forney Lake, Iowa; southern Saskatchewan; North and South Dakota; The Pas, Manitoba; Skagit Flats, Washington; and Horseshoe Lake, Illinois—some of the goose hunting hot spots Cadieux (1986) describes in *Successful Goose Hunting.* And then, of course, there is the Delmarva Peninsula, the place many consider to be *the* goose hunting capital of the world. Across the country, in everything from rusty old pickup trucks to sophisticated small jet planes, hunters journey to the fields, marshes, lakes, and mud flats where geese congregate. They wear old coveralls and rubber boots, expensive Gortex camouflage and leather hunting shoes—and everything in between. They carry the family shotgun used by their grandfathers or the latest fancy Remington autoloader. Goose hunting is the sport of the rich landowner and the poor farmer or waterman. What they all have in common is a passion for goose hunting. Many rate geese at the pinnacle of waterfowl hunting.

Michener writes of the spirit and enthusiasm of the goose hunter in *Chesapeake*. His character Lafe Turlock is a Maryland farmer with a passion for goose: "I can eat it roasted, or chopped with onions and peppers, or sliced thin with mushrooms. You can keep the other months of the year, just give me November with a fat goose comin' onto the stove three times a week. . . . Canniest birds in the world. They have a sixth sense, a seventh and an eighth. I've seen one smart old gander lead his flock right into my blind, spot my gun, stop dead in the air, turn his whole congregation around on a sixpence, without me gettin' a shot. . . . A roast goose tastes so good because it's so danged hard to shoot."

The week before opening of goose season, the whole Chesapeake Eastern Shore bustles with activity. Hunting supply stores are crowded. The marshes and coves are alive with activity as new reeds are cut and placed to hide blinds. New pit blinds are dug and decoy spreads carefully arranged. It seems as if every male in the five counties is a goose hunter. And all of them seem to have severe cases of goose fever.

Goose fever should not be confused with the similar affliction that sometimes accompanies it, decoy fever. Goose fever produces profound changes in behavior for those suffering from the disease. The mildly afflicted may sit for hours observing geese, usually in favorable weather in places where geese are readily accessible. More advanced cases of goose fever lead to much more lengthy time spans devoted to goose mania; inclement weather and arduous trips to locate geese are no deterrent. In serious cases, the afflicted often feels compelled to purchase shotguns and camouflage clothing, and to rent very expensive

goose blinds. It may even lead to the acquisition of a hunting dog.

A variant of the fever leads to the purchase of expensive cameras and lens, as hunters of a different sort—nature photographers and wildlife enthusiasts—outfit themselves for their pursuit of the geese. In either manifestation of the fever, the individual becomes obsessed with geese. He or she rises well before sunup to be in place before the first goose stirs, and sits for long hours waiting for just the right moment to get that perfect shot.

Severe cases of goose fever are often accompanied by marital discord unless the spouse happens to be similarly afflicted. Bumper stickers on many Maryland pickup trucks proclaim "We interrupt this marriage for the duration of the goose season" and "My wife told me she'd leave me if I went goose hunting one more time. . . . I sure am going to miss that woman!" On the positive side, sufferers of goose fever are generally physically healthy, happy, and enthusiastic individuals who very much enjoy life—so long as they can get to their geese.

Decoy fever, as distinguished from goose fever, generally leads the individual to more sedentary indoor activities such as browsing interminably through antique shops looking for old decoys, and attending wildfowl decoy shows and auctions for the purpose of acquiring decoys. A variation of this fever leads the individual to enroll in carving courses; to purchase books, innumerable varieties of wood, and multitudes of carving tools; and in its most serious cases, to compete in carving shows. The sufferer of decoy fever may become as obsessed with geese as the person with a severe case of goose fever. The most dangerous—and most expensive —illness, of course, results from being stricken simultaneously with goose fever and decoy fever!

DISTRIBUTION PROBLEMS IN MAJOR WINTERING AREAS

Data from both Canadian studies and the U.S. Fish and Wildlife Service indicate that Canada Goose numbers are stable or even increasing if the total count of all subspecies across the United States and Canada is considered. Many subspe-

"Frosty Decoys."

Canada Geese landing at Blackwater National Wildlife Refuge, Maryland.

"Three Geese Flying."

cies continue to thrive, primarily because they nest in the arctic tundra where their habitat is fairly secure. These arctic nesting geese are not being pushed out of their nesting habitat by subdivisions, highways, wetlands drained for crops, or pesticide pollution of marshlands. Such problems are affecting duck production very drastically, but are having little impact on the production of Canada Geese since few geese nest in the prairie pothole regions in the Midwest or the farmlands of central Canada.

Exceptions to this rosy picture affect some races of Canada Geese, however. Some subspecies of the Canada Goose are seriously jeopardized. The Aleutian race very nearly became extinct due to fox predation at the nesting sites. The Dusky Canada Goose is not doing well at its nesting area in the Copper River Delta of Alaska. The catastrophe of an oil spill in Prince William Sound has affected nesting geese in that area of Alaska. And should plans go forward to dam the Yukon River, nesting sites for 200,000

Alaskan Geese would be eliminated or seriously reduced.

With the exception of these problems at some Alaskan nesting sites, the production of young goslings throughout most of the Arctic is stable over the long term. Although the total number of goslings hatched each year is relatively stable, major distribution problems affect the populations of Canada Geese that winter in the United States. Waterfowl resource managers at both the state and federal level report the concentration of too many geese in some states with too few in other states with good wintering habitat.

Texas, Louisiana, Alabama, Mississippi, New Mexico, and North Carolina all had sizable wintering flocks of geese sixty years ago, according to Cadieux (1986). Now these states see very few geese. Take the case of Mattamuskeet, North Carolina: Lake Mattamuskeet was acquired by the federal government in 1934 and turned into a national wildlife refuge for waterfowl. In 1935, the refuge held some 12,000 geese. By 1958

A Delaware wildlife refuge.

105,000 wintered there, and as many as 131,000 by 1968. But suddenly in 1969, the numbers of geese at Mattamuskeet declined drastically, and in subsequent years dropped even further.

Bosque Del Apache and other refuges in New Mexico once had large numbers of Canada Geese wintering over in their marshes. Now the majority of that portion of the Highline Population of geese remain farther north in eastern Colorado, mostly in the city of Denver and its suburbs.

The entire Atlantic Population of Canada Geese has declined in numbers in the past five years, according to the annual surveys conducted by the U.S. Fish and Wildlife Service. In January 1983, estimates for Canada Geese wintering from New England to North Carolina totaled 889,000. In 1984, the number had dropped to 822,000; by 1988 the estimate was 738,000; and for 1989 only 661,000. Between 1983 and 1989, the Atlantic Population of Canada Geese decreased 26 percent.

This decline is especially visible in Maryland and Delaware, where hunters and state wildlife managers are very much concerned about the shrinking goose population. The midwinter count dropped in Maryland from a high in 1981 of 600,700 geese to a low in January of 1989 of 263,000, according to the Maryland Department of Natural Resources. That represents a 56 percent decline in wintering geese. While everyone agrees that fewer geese winter in Maryland and Delaware, how to reverse these declining numbers generates considerable controversy.

WHY DISTRIBUTION PATTERNS CHANGE

Why have large numbers of geese shifted their winter homes to locations farther north in the past decade or so? No one is certain. A number of theories attempt to account for waterfowl distribution; each seems to have some validity.

One theory holds that warmer winters may encourage shortstopping among geese, that is,

A Canada Goose feeding.

staying farther north than they normally would in colder winters. Open water for resting and sleeping is very important to geese as well as to other waterfowl. When the more northerly ponds and lakes remain open, some geese linger there rather than head farther south to more traditional wintering quarters.

Certainly farming practices and the ready availability of favored food supplies are a factor also. Geese are highly adaptive in their feeding habits. They have a marked preference for grains, cereals, and green forage grown by humans. One study in southern Illinois showed that cornfields attracted 41 percent of the geese in the area, small-grain fields 24 percent, pasture 22 percent, and soybeans 9 percent. In Colorado, geese feed primarily on green winter wheat fields in the southeast. Geese also eat native plants such as spike rush, American bulrush, and native grasses (Bellrose 1976). On the Delmarva Peninsula, wintering geese favor corn, although they also spend much time in winter wheat fields.

In general, the theories explaining distribution problems all point to changes impacting the wintering geese and their winter habitat, in contrast to the relative stability the geese experience on their nesting grounds. Many of these changes are wrought by the year-round residents of the geese's wintering grounds, people. Some changes invite the geese to winter in a particular area; others decimate populations and discourage recovery.

Why geese change their wintering homes from time to time seems best explained by considering each particular case in question. In Colorado, for example, apparently the non-migrating local flock of Canada Geese has greatly expanded in the past ten years due to the "refuge effect" provided by the city of Denver and its suburbs. The resident geese have thrived on a diet of lawn, golf course, and park grasses, without having to endure the dangers of being shot. When the migrating flocks pass through the area, apparently the local geese act as decoys. The migrants, in turn, find the area hospitable and safe from hunting, so they tend to remain there for the winter, rather than heading down to the New Mexico marshes.

In North Carolina, the shift in goose wintering quarters seems to have occurred for entirely different reasons. In 1969, most of the 131,000 Canada Geese that had previously wintered at Lake Mattamuskeet, North Carolina during the 1960s disappeared. It was as if they had all sold their beach-front cottages in North Carolina and bought new condos on Maryland's Eastern Shore! Very heavy hunting pressure and large harvests of geese took place at Lake Mattamuskeet during the 1960s. A number of wildlife managers believe that heavy harvests, combined with a changing age structure of the flock, are primary factors in reducing the size of wintering flocks.

Ready availability of food may have been a contributing factor to the shift of the Lake Mattamuskeet goose population as well. Apparently, the geese thought the corn and soybeans in Maryland were easier picking than the crops being grown in North Carolina. The farming practices in both areas were changing at the time the geese moved north. The North Carolina farmers were growing earlier varieties of corn that they harvested well before the geese arrived. The Maryland farmers at the same time were adding more corn and soybeans to their fields and building ponds.

Interestingly, in the past several years, the geese seem to be shifting farther north in Maryland to upper Queen Anne, Kent, and Cecil counties. Dorchester and Talbot counties to the south have had fewer geese each year. Again, easy corn picking may be the main factor accounting for the shift. But there are also increased numbers of small ponds in the northern counties. These new ponds, combined with warmer winters that have kept the water open, may have added to the attractions farther north.

Overzealous hunting is thought to be the reason for population shifts in other parts of the country, as well. Waterfowl managers and hunters in Missouri, for example, believe that their more enlightened hunting regulations were responsible for the increase in their wintering flocks at the same time the Texas and Louisiana flocks were declining. The Missourians believe that the southern states allowed such large har-

A frosty morning in the cornfield.

vests each year that eventually too few breeding birds were left to make the flights to the nesting grounds and back. They feel that the proportionally smaller harvest of the Missouri flocks allowed this group to increase significantly in numbers.

POLLUTED REFUGES AND SHRINKING WETLANDS

Another major reason for changes in goose distribution during the winter relates to the drastic decline in wetlands that has occurred in both the United States and Canada in the past several decades. In the late 1800s, vast numbers of waterfowl—ducks, Canada Geese, and snow geese—migrated through the prairie pothole regions of the Dakotas according to reports from hunters of that era. Hunters easily shot ten or twenty geese in an hour from the thousands surrounding them. Now many prairie potholes have been drained for farming, significantly reducing the waterfowl habitat in what used to be a veritable paradise of "duck factories."

The loss of wetland waterfowl habitat in California has reached extreme proportions. The skies over the central valley of California once were filled with wintering waterfowl, according to Peter Steinhart (1987) in an article titled "Empty the Skies" written for *Audubon Magazine*. Just a few years ago, California was host to 60 percent of the Pacific Flyway's wintering ducks and geese: 40 percent of the flyway's Cackling Canada Geese, 72 percent of the white-fronted geese, and 84 percent of the pintail ducks. Now the huge flocks of geese and ducks have almost vanished along with the wetlands. The state once had 5 million acres of wetlands; now 92 percent of those marshes are gone. The marshes have been drained for farming, houses, highways, airports, military bases, and garbage dumps. In the central valley, 96 percent of the wetlands have disappeared, leaving very few habitable spaces for waterfowl. In the San Francisco Bay area, 75 percent of the original tidal marshes are gone along with the bald eagles, peregrine falcons, and numerous other species that once frequented the coastal wetlands.

In addition to the huge losses of waterfowl habitat in California, the quality of the remaining wetlands has also declined. One national wildlife refuge set up to protect habitat for ducks and geese has turned out to be deadly poisonous. Kesterson National Wildlife Refuge was built from ponds originally designed to hold waste water drained from farms surrounding the area. The Bureau of Reclamation of the Department of Interior had built a number of irrigation projects in central California in the 1970s. It planned a large concrete drainage ditch from the east side of the San Joaquin Valley to San Francisco Bay. This long ditch was to drain off the alkali water collected in perforated pipes just above the impervious layer of clay under the farmers' fields. When the Bureau of Reclamation ran out of money to complete the drainage ditch, it built holding ponds for the farm waste water. These ponds were later turned into Kesterson National Wildlife Refuge, despite warnings from a number of environmentally concerned groups that farm waste water was dangerous to wildlife (Steinhart 1987; Carter 1988).

Several years after the refuge opened, dead and deformed birds did indeed begin to appear in the ponds. The plants and invertebrates eaten by the waterfowl in the refuge were found to contain toxic amounts of selenium, arsenic, and boron. The state of California declared Kesterson National Wildlife Refuge a toxic pit in 1985 and ordered the Department of the Interior to clean up the refuge or close it within three years. In March 1985, a few days after the disaster at Kesterson aired as a feature story on CBS's "60 Minutes" news broadcast, Interior Secretary Hodel ordered the refuge closed. At this writing in mid-1989, the federal agency has implemented no clean-up plan yet, and thousands of birds continue to use the area and die as a result. No one wants to fund the clean-up costs, and disagreement about how to handle the problem effectively prevents solution.

In the meanwhile, with no feasible solution to the problems at Kesterson National Wildlife Refuge, it is becoming increasingly evident that many other refuges are similarly endangered. Twenty-one refuges or wetlands areas are currently being investigated for drainage water pollution. And many more wetlands and refuges in Wyoming, Utah, Texas, Nevada, and Arizona, as well as a number of areas in California, may be poisoned by agricultural waste water (Carter 1988).

HUNTING REGULATION AS A MANAGEMENT TOOL

Because the main cause of early mortality in Canada Geese is hunting, the role of hunting regulations is critical to preserving the species. Hunting regulations are designed to ensure the survival of game animals including waterfowl at optimum levels, so that each species may maintain its numbers through reproduction. Hunting laws are also designed to influence the distribution of wildlife.

Waterfowl biologists believe that 85 to 90 percent of goose mortality in fall comes from harvest or crippling loss caused by hunters. Death due to disease has not been a big factor for geese. And since nesting habitat for most Canada Geese is relatively secure in regions of the Arctic that are undeveloped, the reproduction rate for geese is not a concern. Ducks have suffered a severe decline in production because their nesting habitat has been greatly reduced. But Canada Geese continue to reproduce at a high rate, provided enough breeding birds reach the nesting grounds each year. Late snow cover at the nesting sites seems to be the main factor causing fluctuations in gosling reproduction from year to year.

Because of growing concern about the decline in waterfowl in the late 1940s, at the 1951 meeting of the International Association of Game, Fish, and Conservation Commissioners, the waterfowl flyway councils were established. Four flyway councils were set up, corresponding to the major waterfowl flyways: Atlantic, Mississippi, Central, and Pacific, each with a number of voting members, including the directors of the respective fish and game departments for the states within the flyway. The four flyway councils review data and make their recommendations each year on hunting regulations for all species of waterfowl in the flyways. Two delegates from each council present their recommendations to the director of the U.S. Fish and Wildlife Service, Department of the Interior, at the annual August meeting of the Waterfowl Advisory Committee. The views of various private, nongovernmental organizations such as Ducks Unlimited, the National Wildlife Federation, the Audubon Society, the Wildlife Management Institute, and others concerned about waterfowl are also presented at the August meeting. Following these meetings, the director of the Fish and Wildlife Service sets the harvest limit for each species.

Once the federal hunting regulations for each species are published, each state then determines whether it will accept the federal guidelines, or pass more restrictive limits for its hunters. The states may not issue more liberal regulations than the federal regulations, but they are free to tighten the numbers for harvest if they desire. According to Hawkins (1976), in a chapter titled "The Role of Hunting Regulations," "regulations are used to provide recreational opportunities and distribute and limit the size of the harvest. . . . Generally, the flyways have differing regulations designed to distribute recreational opportunities and harvest in relation to migrational patterns of the birds, hunting pressure exerted against them, or both. Flyway hunting regulations generally can be progressively more liberal as the proportion of migrating birds harvested by hunters decreases."

THE MARYLAND BAG LIMIT CONTROVERSY, 1988–89 SEASON

A hornet's nest of controversy swarmed around the Maryland Department of Natural Resources (DNR) when it decided to impose stricter hunting limits for Canada Geese than those required by the U.S. Fish and Wildlife Service for the 1988–89 season. The federal guidelines for Maryland, Delaware, and Virginia for Canada Geese in the Atlantic Flyway were no more than two geese per day in a seventy-day season. The state of Maryland imposed a bag limit of one goose per day for the first fourteen days of the season and two birds per day for the remaining portion of a sixty-day goose season. In the prior two years, Maryland had a bag limit of three geese per day, with a seventy-day sea-

A prairie pothole in North Dakota.

Canada Geese landing in a snowstorm.

Canada Geese in the Chesapeake marshes.

son. (Neighboring Delaware established a two-bird limit with a sixty-day season for 1988–89.)

As soon as rumors suggested that Maryland might issue more restrictive regulations than the federal guidelines permitted, the battle lines were drawn. On the one side gathered the hunting guides, outfitters, and other commercial interests such as hotel and restaurant owners who feared drastic income losses from greatly reduced numbers of hunters coming to the Eastern Shore that year. On the other side were the Department of Natural Resources personnel, conservationists, and hunters who were concerned that the federal guidelines were not strict enough to effectively reduce the harvest of adult birds in Maryland. Neither side seemed to dispute the considerable drop in the numbers of wintering Canada Geese in Maryland and Delaware in the past few years. But differences about how to correct the situation and when action should have been taken caused much heated controversy. Disagreement about why the numbers of geese are dropping on

the Delmarva Peninsula added to the difficulty of finding common ground for discussion. And there was also some question about the accuracy of the official estimates of goose populations and the numbers harvested.

Larry Albright, owner of Albright's Gun Shop in Easton, Maryland and chairman of the Talbot County Ducks Unlimited Chapter, in a letter to the Maryland governor, wrote of his concerns about the more restrictive hunting limits. There had been strong support among the hunters two years earlier for reducing the daily bag limit then from three to two geese in order to limit the harvest, wrote Albright. He and other hunters were angry that positive action had not been taken two years earlier. They felt such action would have eliminated the need for dropping the limit to one bird at the start of the 1988–89 season. Albright also asserted that the state could have done more to cooperate with the federal Fish and Wildlife Service in keeping more geese at the Blackwater National Wildlife Refuge in lower Maryland. He further suggested that the state should create more sanctuary space for geese on the Eastern Shore.

Five days before the regulations for Maryland's hunting season were set for 1988, a public meeting organized by the DNR took place in Easton, Maryland. According to reports published in the local newspapers, several hundred people attended that public meeting, almost none of who supported the one-goose limit. The Maryland Waterfowl Outfitters Association brought suit against the Department of Natural Resources to try to stop the one-bird bag limit. Legislation was introduced to restrict the state from setting more stringent regulations than those published by the federal authorities. Some people questioned the accuracy of the harvest count. Others questioned the estimates of geese wintering in the state, or felt that the count had dropped because geese were shortstopping farther north in Pennsylvania and New Jersey.

While some opposed the DNR's restrictive hunting regulations, many conservation-minded hunters, guides, and farmers were concerned that failure to take decisive action to lower the harvest rate in Maryland would lead to a repeat of the great losses in goose population experienced by North Carolina in the late 1960s. They agreed with the state that reducing the bag limit from three geese to two might not significantly lower the harvest. And indeed, in one state where the daily bag limit was reduced by one bird, the harvest was actually higher for that year than it had been for the prior year. Apparently, the hunters simply went out more days because of the slightly lowered bag limit.

This all seems like a tremendous amount of controversy for a difference between one or two birds per day for fourteen days, less than one-fourth of the entire hunting season. But the reason for all the furor appears to be that fully half the birds harvested for the entire hunting season are shot in the opening two weeks of the season. This high proportion of the harvest early in the season seems to come about for several reasons. The first few days of the season, it is easier to shoot the young naive birds before they become wary of hunters. Second, most hunters go out early in the season when their chances are better for bagging their geese and when the weather is better. The commercial outfitters and guides were convinced that few out-of-state hunters would come to Maryland with a one-goose bag limit for the opening of the season. Hunters pay from $100 to $200 a day to hunt with a guide. Farmers who lease their farms to commercial hunting guides may earn as much as $20,000 a season for a good "goose farm." These people all feared a loss of income as a result of the DNR decision. And indeed, some out-of-state hunters canceled their trips when the one-goose limit for the season opening was announced.

From the perspective of the Maryland Department of Natural Resources, Larry Hindman, the Migratory Bird Program manager, defended his tough decision with the facts as he saw them. He noted the decline since 1983 in geese for the Atlantic Population, but added that the drop for Maryland was even greater. His figures indicated a decrease of 35 to 40 percent in the geese wintering in Maryland since the high point of the mid-1970s. At the same time, hunters harvested an increased number of birds in Maryland. In the early 1960s, hunters killed less than 20 percent of the fall flight, while in the past several years they have taken 30 percent or more of the fall flight. Not only are more hunters shooting geese in Maryland, but the hunters are more successful in bagging geese than they used to be. Newer techniques such as the use of stuffed taxidermy birds as decoys and flagging with moving cloth or cardboard wing-like "flags" to attract passing geese have greatly increased the harvest. Another significant factor increasing the success of hunters is the commercial management of hunting farms. With large areas leased and controlled by one guide service, the hunting parties can be moved from field to field on successive days. Since geese avoid fields where they have recently experienced shooting, having a number of prime feeding and resting locations available for hunting gives the hunters a great advantage.

Hindman was concerned about the escalating overharvest of geese. He pointed out the long-term effects of the overhunting of young geese: Too many future breeders were being shot. Recent studies by Hardy and Tacha (1989) indicate that most Canada Geese do not begin to breed until they are three years old, and many do not breed until their fifth year. Studies of recovered banded Canada Geese give evidence that the majority of birds die before their tenth year. Only a few survive to their fifteenth or twentieth year.

Ron Reynolds, of the U.S. Fish and Wildlife Service, thinks that the bottom line is this: High hunting pressure reduces the number of young geese who survive to an age of high reproductive potential (five years). The population of older geese is not replenished at the same rate as it is being lost. Consequently, the average age of breeding adults falls lower than is desirable, and the goose population is less productive overall.

The Maryland DNR sought to decrease especially the number of young geese killed by greatly reducing the bag limit during the early part of the hunting season when more young geese are shot. With regard to the one-goose limit for the opening fourteen days, Hindman was convinced that dropping from three to two birds would not have had any significant effect on the harvest numbers. That is the primary reason why the DNR had not cut the limit to two birds in the earlier years. The experience of other states in reducing the limit by one-third was that the hunters adjusted to the two bag limit by going hunting more often. The harvest numbers remained high as a result. The Maryland authorities decided that it was better to have some decline in income for the hunting interests now rather than risk a continued decline in the size of the Maryland flocks such as happened in North and South Carolina, Texas, and Louisiana.

To test the accuracy of the numbers used by the Maryland DNR to conclude that more young geese were being harvested, a private nonprofit group, the Chesapeake Wildlife Heritage, was asked to conduct a survey during the 1987–88 and 1988–89 seasons to assess more accurately the ages of birds shot. Roland Limpert, a research biologist with Chesapeake Wildlife Heritage, studied over 2,000 birds harvested to determine their ages. Using the wing coverts plus the tail feathers gave a slightly more accurate reading of

the birds' ages than using tail feathers alone. Limpert indeed found an increase between the two years in the numbers of young birds harvested.

H. Lloyd Alexander, manager of the Wildlife Section for the Delaware Division of Fish and Wildlife, agrees with Hindman's conclusions about the decline of geese in the two states. Alexander believes his data also support the theory that the drop in goose numbers is caused by overharvesting. The theory that numbers of the Maryland and Delaware geese are shortstopping in Pennsylvania and New Jersey appears reasonable since obviously more Canada geese are in those two states than were there ten years ago. But Alexander states that neck collar studies of birds banded in Delaware show that these geese are not stopping off farther north, but in fact are being shot in Delaware. In the mid-1970s, Delaware had 22,000 adult geese wintering over. In 1988, only 12,000 adult geese wintered in the state. Alexander believes that the instinct to return to the traditional wintering quarters is very strong and that the vast majority of Canada Geese consistently return to their usual winter homes. The increasing numbers of New Jersey and Pennsylvania geese are the result of reproducing local or nonmigrating geese in combination with growth of the flocks of migratory geese who have traditionally wintered in those states. Since there are fewer hunters in those two states than in Maryland and Delaware, according to Alexander, the harvest rates are much lower. The lower harvest rate enables the size of the migrating flocks to grow in those two states. (Counting nonmigrating geese is difficult. There have recently been studies of the growth rate of local geese in the Atlantic Flyway, but the findings so far are only preliminary.)

Reducing the bag limit to significantly lower the harvest rate apparently worked for Maryland. Figures compiled from hunter surveys in Maryland indicated a reduction in the 1988–89 harvest rate to 21 percent compared to a harvest rate of more than 30 percent in the several preceeding years. Apparently lowering the daily bag limit to one bird for the first quarter of the season achieved close to the targeted 20 percent that Maryland wildlife managers hoped to ob-

Canada Geese on the farm at dusk.

tain. They believe that a 20 percent harvest rate will prevent the continued declining trend in the size of the Maryland goose flocks. Most likely, the one-goose limit for the early part of the season will be continued in Maryland for several more years, especially since spring 1989 was an exceptionally poor year for gosling production in the Hudson Bay region. Very late snow cover on the Ungava Peninsula caused a severe drop in nesting success for the Canada Geese in the northeast Hudson Bay region. Maryland's 1989-90 hunting season was reduced to fifty days, with bag limits of one goose per day for the first ten days and two geese per day for the remaining forty days.

SANCTUARY FROM HUNTING

Geese need areas where they can feed and rest without fear of being shot or disturbed. Both land and water are used for loafing and sleeping, although night resting is usually done on open water. The areas of refuge — ponds, marshes, and unhunted lands — must be near large fields with good food supplies. Geese also need fresh water for drinking.

In the Chesapeake region, Canada Geese tend to eat green plants such as winter wheat and aquatic plants in the fall. Later in the winter, the geese prefer more energy-producing foods such as corn and soybeans, although they much favor the corn. In the spring, just prior to migration, many geese consume winter wheat or other green crops. Studies of goose feeding patterns in North Carolina suggest that geese there tend to prefer wheat and alfalfa fields rather than corn fields throughout the entire wintering season. Apparently, in the relatively warmer winters of the Carolinas, high-energy foods such as corn are not as important as they are for the geese wintering on the Delmarva Peninsula.

Wherever geese feed and rest during the day, they are wary of predators. Since wildlife refuges often do not offer enough food for geese, they must fly elsewhere to feed. They leave the refuge

Canada Geese dropping into a harbor of refuge.

The sentinels keep watch. (Photo by Jan Lucie)

or water where they spend the night soon after sunrise, flying in small groups to the feeding grounds. Even though they leave in small groups, eventually the whole flock arrives at the same field to eat and rest during the day. Geese prefer large fields and wide-open spaces for good visibility. While part of the flock feeds or rests, others stand guard. The sentinels keep close watch on both the ground and the sky around them, sounding a loud alarm if they see anything suspicious.

Too much hunting pressure on geese causes them to move to areas with fewer hunters. Geese feed in different fields, avoiding places where they have recently been shot. The birds are very much aware of safe haven areas, crowding the wildlife refuges and frequenting fields where no hunting is allowed. During days of heavy hunting, many geese rest on the water in rivers, lakes, and bays out of range of the hunters' guns. River coves surrounded by houses are favorite resting places early in the hunting season when large

numbers of hunters are out in the fields. Geese also fly at much higher altitudes during the hunting season than they normally would fly.

The majority of hunters are intelligent, conservation-minded people who genuinely care about preserving wildlife. They appreciate the need for bag limits and for areas of sanctuary for the birds. One such hunter on Maryland's Eastern Shore is William Price who manages a goose-hunting guide service. Price also farms for the geese. Every year, he raises thousands of dollars worth of corn and sorghum for the geese. He spends $150 to $200 a month in the winter to keep his pond from freezing over so that the geese may have open water for resting and drinking, no matter how cold the winter. On days when other ponds in the area are frozen over, he will have from 5,000 to 10,000 geese on his farm, which he patrols from dawn to dusk to prevent hunters from straying onto his goose sanctuary. He told me about one day in January several years ago when there was a great deal of

Geese gliding into a sanctuary on hunting day.

hunting in the area. The geese came winging in to his farm by the thousands that day until they covered his driveway, his front and back lawns, and the entire area of fields and pond. He called the local game wardens for help with protecting what they estimated to be 50,000 geese that descended to his farm for sanctuary that day!

Many waterfowl hunters belong to Ducks Unlimited, a nonprofit conservation organization dedicated to preserving waterfowl habitat. Ducks Unlimited has over 550,000 members who care enough about preserving waterfowl to contribute large sums of money for the purchase and development of wetlands. Since the formation of the organization in 1937, Ducks Unlimited has raised nearly one-half billion dollars in support of waterfowl! Sportsmen and women such as these become very upset with hunters who disobey the laws designed to protect and preserve the species.

"GAME LAWS WEREN'T WRIT FOR FAT CATS"

Unfortunately for the geese, some hunters use illegal methods for attracting waterfowl such as baiting fields or rivers with corn and grain. Others shoot more than the legal limit of birds, or shoot on days when the hunting season is closed. Illegal hunting is a serious problem in many parts of the United States, including Maryland, as Willie J. Parker, a retired Federal Fish and Wildlife agent, documents in his fascinating book *Game Warden: Chesapeake Assignment.*

In 1966, I discovered, and made known to all concerned, that the hunting public in Maryland had a hearty contempt for federal regulations and the people that enforced them. It was apparent at this time that it was imperative that we launch an intensive law enforcement effort that was designed to change the attitude of

44

Resting in the snow.

the hunting public and stop the loss of birds by illegal hunting. This loss in 1966 was frightening. It was estimated by concerned knowledgeable people to be as much as eighty percent of the total kill. *(emphasis added)*

Parker attributed the almost total obliteration of canvasback ducks from the Chesapeake Bay to illegal hunting. Unlike Canada Geese, canvasbacks will keep on returning to baited waters until the last duck in the flock is shot. Geese at least have sense enough to avoid areas where they have been heavily hunted in recent days.

The number of game wardens available to enforce state and federal hunting regulations is often completely inadequate to stop violations. Sometimes strong political pressures discourage the arrest of V.I.P lawbreakers. As recently as 1988, the former manager of the Blackwater National Wildlife Refuge in Cambridge, Maryland was transferred elsewhere for zealous pursuit of poaching hunters around the refuge, according to Ted Williams (1989) in his article "Game Laws Weren't Writ for Fat Cats." Since Maryland's Eastern Shore offers the closest waterfowl hunting to the District of Columbia, a number of politicians and government officials hunt there. Don Perkuchin took over management of the Blackwater Refuge in 1984. He decided to ignore the old custom of looking the other way when V.I.P.s violated the hunting laws, and began arresting everyone he caught shooting in baited fields. Because some of those he arrested included several congressmen and some influential lobbyists, word came down from on high that he was to be transferred. His two immediate superiors supported him and refused to fire him. As a result, all three men were transferred to other jobs in 1988, according to Williams.

Willie Parker experienced the same kind of

pressure to look the other way when influential people broke the hunting laws. As federal special agent in charge of the Maryland and Virginia District between 1966 and 1974, he experienced numerous attempts to influence his arrests. Parker and his agents effectively arrested and brought to trial both rich and poor for illegal hunting. Due to careful preparation and hard work on the part of Parker and his agents, the vast majority of their cases resulted in convictions. He frequently got calls from representatives, senators, influential lawyers, and state officials seeking deals to get their friends off. In 1972, Parker received information from several sources that his transfer out of the state was imminent. He had ruffled too many important feathers in his relentless pursuit of violators. They were going to get him this time. He immediately wrote a long letter to his supervisor, detailing his service and accomplishments, noting that he had hired a lawyer and intended to fight any transfer or dismissal attempt. As a result of this action, Parker was left alone for two more years. When the supervisory job above him became open, he applied for the vacancy. This would have made him agent in charge of law enforcement for District Eleven, an area that included Maryland. He was not selected for that job, the only one he had applied for. Instead, he was appointed agent in charge of District Ten, headquartered in Nashville, Kentucky (Parker 1983).

Was Parker's effective and impartial pursuit of lawbreakers an embarrassment to the Department of Interior? Was he moved out of the Chesapeake area so the fat cats could pursue their illegal baiting and slaughter of waterfowl without having to worry about being arrested?

A canvasback duck emerging from a dive. Reduced numbers of canvasbacks in Maryland's Chesapeake Bay area may be because of illegal hunting.

SPRING: MATES FOR LIFE

Canada Geese form a lifelong pair bond once they have mated. This pair bond is so strong that a goose or gander will endanger itself to find and help an injured mate. One finding from a recent study by Roland Limpert of the Chesapeake Wildlife Heritage suggests that geese may go through a severe mourning period when they lose a mate. In his study, Limpert put neck collars on over 200 geese, including both goose and gander in several pairs, as well as a number of individual geese. In the case of three collared pairs, one bird from each pair was shot that season, and within ten days, the remaining bird from each pair was also shot! It may be that wearing the neck collars made these particular geese more vulnerable or more attractive to hunters. But it may also be true that birds who have lost their mates are more vulnerable. Field observations indicated that the surviving birds spent much time calling and searching for their mates, staying at the edge of the flock or even leaving the flock to extend the range of their search. Such behavior apparently increases the vulnerability of the survivor of the pair.

We might also speculate that the surviving mate suffers some kind of emotional depression just as bereaved people do when they lose a loved one. We know from other animal studies that lonely and depressed animals often neither eat nor take care of themselves well. It would not be too surprising if depression were a factor in the increased vulnerability of geese who have lost a mate. Anyone who has observed a lone goose searching and honking for its mate can hear the stressed, mournful sounds of the calling. When the injured mate dies or cannot be found, a goose will form a new pair bond before the next breeding season, or within a few days if the loss of the mate occurs just before breeding season.

PAIR BONDING AND COURTSHIP

Young Canada ganders choose mates when they reach the age of two or three years. The pairs are usually about the same age, and the goose is smaller than the gander. This pair bonding takes place after the flock migrates to the nesting ground. Previously formed pairs can be seen flying close together as the flocks move to and from their feeding grounds on the winter range. The pair may fly in unison with the same wing positions, one bird just above and slightly behind the other. On land and on the water, the two stay very close together when feeding or resting.

When a gander has chosen his goose, he will defend the territory around her, driving away other potential suitors. There may be brief fights over the goose, but often threat displays are sufficient to keep other ganders away. To give the mildest warning display, a gander pumps his head up and down. Responding to a more serious situation, he extends his head forward and rotates it vigorously, waving the head and neck back and forth. In the full attack, the gander

Pairs of geese flying in unison.

Overleaf: An aggressive gander.

stretches his neck out horizontally straight toward his opponent, hissing as he swims or runs at his rival.

Full courtship display and copulation take place for the first time only when the geese have formed the pair bond, as Stokes (1979) describes:

Once the two are committed to each other, they frequently perform the Greeting Ceremony.

The Greeting Ceremony occurs between mates or family members that have just come together after being apart. . . . In the ceremony the male alternates the Snore-call with the Ahonk-call and its accompanying Rolling display. At the same time, the female holds her neck in a diagonal position and gives her Hink-call. . . .

A feature of the display that is hard to believe even after you have heard it is that the male Ahonk-call and female Hink-call are given as a duet. Each alternates with the other in such a perfectly timed way that together they sound like one call. . . .

. . . The main precopulatory display is Neck-dipping. In this the birds rhythmically dip their heads and necks deep into the water and toss water over their backs as they bring them out. During the display the male aligns himself alongside the female and finally steps onto her back while holding her neck feathers in his bill. After copulation, both birds do Head-up. Throughout the Neck-dipping phase, both birds tread water with their feet, stirring it up on the sides.

In the rolling display, part of the greeting between the courting pair, the male or female shakes and tosses its head with the bill pointed up and the neck stretched up at its mate. The bird shakes its head slowly or more vigorously to the point of strongly waving its head and neck in arcs. More vigorous head shaking is accompanied by strident honking (Palmer 1976). The head-up position refers to a behavior frequently seen after mating: On the water, the pair of geese together extend their necks and lift their heads up, tipping them back slightly (Stokes 1979).

MIGRATION TO NESTING GROUNDS

The spring migration of Canada Geese is not as spectacular as the fall flight since the geese travel in smaller groups over a longer period of time on their way to the nesting grounds. In the far south, people have seen movement north as early as late January, but in the middle latitudes of the United States, it is late February or early March before the geese begin to leave. While there seems to be some gathering together of large flocks prior to migration, it is not the mass staging that occurs in the fall migration.

During the spring migration, many flocks travel leisurely, perhaps covering only ten miles or so per day at first (Palmer 1976). What prompts the flocks to leave the winter range in small groups is not known. It has been suggested that as the migration progresses, more territory is covered each day. The geese often make the very last leg of the journey over the northern Canadian forests in one nonstop trip. Most of the geese appear to arrive at their home nesting grounds at the same time.

NESTING

Geese arrive at the nesting ground in flocks consisting largely of family units with the goose, the gander, and the yearlings hatched the previous year. The flock also contains juveniles two or three years old that are not yet ready to breed and individuals that have lost their mates or for some reason have not formed pair bonds. By the time the flock reaches the nesting territory, those birds that are going to breed already have established their pair bonds and completed courtship and copulation so that they arrive in egg-laying condition ready to build nests.

Pairs that have nested the previous year usually reclaim the same nest site. Newly formed pairs of breeders take whatever space is left over for their nests. Since the ganders become very territorial shortly before nest building begins, a period of conflict over nest sites starts soon after the flock arrives. The gander chases all birds away from the immediate area of the nest site, including the yearlings. The yearlings and juveniles, therefore, gather together at the edges of the nesting territory. Juveniles sometimes mimic their elders by trying out pair bonding, often with considerable altercation among themselves. They "play" with nesting materials and

Dusky Canada Goose nesting area in the Copper River Delta, Alaska. (Photo by U.S. Fish and Wildlife Service)

occasionally even build nests. One study, in which a number of juvenile birds were marked, found that the young prebreeding pairs "playing house" returned to build nests and raise families at the same sites the following spring.

When plenty of suitable nesting habitat is available, as it usually is in the arctic tundra, the nests of Canada Geese will be well separated. If late snow cover reduces the available habitat, the nests will be closer together. Geese are very adaptable, making the best of difficult nesting conditions. Several studies of nesting sites used by local geese in California, Idaho, and Michigan suggest that when necessary, as many as thirty geese may nest on half an acre. Observers reported four geese nesting on an island twelve by thirty feet in the Snake River in Idaho. Another reported counted eleven goose nests on a large haystack in Oregon (Palmer 1976).

Biologists disagree about which one of the pair selects the nesting site. The majority seem to favor the goose as primary in selecting the site.

The chosen site must have fresh growing grasses nearby for food, and it must be close to water. Geese favor small islands as nesting sites because they are easily defended. The nest site must be high enough so that it will not be flooded by spring rains or snow melt. There must also be wide visibility from the nest in all directions. Geese do not count on camouflage or concealment for protection the way many species do.

Some Giant Canada Geese nesting in Missouri have a most unusual nesting territory. On a 100-mile stretch of the Missouri River near St. Charles, limestone cliffs rise 200 feet above the river. Denver Bryan (1987), in a lovely photo essay published in *Birder's World*, shows the Giant Canadas nesting on ledges high up on the cliffs. On the day following hatching, the adults fly to the bottom of the cliffs, calling their goslings to follow. The baby goslings must jump onto the rocks and shrubs below, sometimes as far as 100 feet. Having survived the jump, the little goslings then must struggle across railroad tracks

53

Goslings preparing to jump from their cliffside nest to the river below. (Photo by Denver Bryan)

Canada Goose rearranging the down in her nest.

Brooding the goslings.

to reach the river. Almost all of them complete the incredible journey to the river.

In the event that part of the traditional nesting territory is covered with late snow or is flooded so that the birds compete for nesting space, the older pairs assert their rights to the territory. Apparently age has its privileges among geese! If any birds must go without a suitable nesting site, it is the newly formed young pairs. Therefore, when suitable nesting habitat is limited, few prebreeders become breeders that year, thus reducing the numbers of goslings hatched (Palmer 1976).

Once the nest site has been selected, the gander drives away all intruders while the female builds the nest. The goose begins building her nest two or three days before she lays eggs. She hollows out a depression in the ground which she then lines with material from the immediate vicinity. She may use sticks and small stones, grasses, or whatever is nearby. Goose nests are not elaborate constructions, but are fairly simple hollows with a small amount of lining material built up around the edge of the nest. The finishing touch is goose down, which she plucks from her breast.

Goose nests in lower Canada and the United States vary considerably, according to the site chosen and materials available. In marshy areas, geese often build nests on top of muskrat houses. The high dome-shaped structures afford good visibility and security from high water. Geese also use tree stumps, platforms, and other structures supplied by humans for nests.

Once the nest is completed, the goose lays four to seven creamy white eggs, occasionally more. The egg-laying period may take six days. When the last egg has been deposited in the nest, the goose begins the incubation. She remains on the nest for twenty-six to twenty-eight days, except for brief periods when she leaves to feed. The goose takes a rest from sitting on the nest early in the morning and later in the day to feed, drink, bathe, and preen. The gander stands close by her during this break. If the nest is surrounded by snow, the goose does not leave the nest to feed.

While incubating the eggs, the goose has a routine of stereotyped movements that she per-forms every fifty minutes or so. She stands up, turns the eggs with her bill, settles down again, paddles with her feet to turn the eggs into position, then pulls at the nesting material on the rim with her bill, and maybe adds to the nest a little new material from nearby (Palmer 1976). There are reports of ganders sitting on the nest, especially toward hatching time. But the majority of the incubation is done by the goose. The gander remains close by the nest, within thirty yards or so throughout the nesting period. Just prior to hatching, the gander moves in closer to guard the family. Once the goslings have hatched, he no longer defends the nest territory, but he and the goose guard and defend the goslings wherever they go.

With geese, as with other waterfowl, a puzzling phenomenon sometimes happens after the young hatch. The broods of goslings may mix, and the goslings may be combined into rearing groups called crèches with ten to twenty goslings under the care of a single set of adults. No solid data exists to explain why this phenomenon occurs.

Bellrose (1976) notes that when the nesting space is limited so that many nests are crowded into a small area, as happens in the western states sometimes, the broods of newly hatched goslings may become mixed up for a brief time. Apparently neither the goslings nor the adults can recognize each other during the first couple of weeks. One study found that mixing of broods ended around three weeks after hatching, while another study indicated it could go on until the sixth week before everyone was sorted out into their original families. Perhaps the parents' inability to recognize their own hatchlings accounts for the phenomenon of the rearing groups. But other studies suggest that young breeding females give up their goslings to older birds for raising (Palmer 1976).

FACTORS AFFECTING GOSLING PRODUCTION

Canada Geese reach their nesting grounds in the northern reaches of Canada in middle to late May and early June. For these geese, the production of goslings depends on several factors, especially the weather, according to Ron Reynolds of the U.S. Fish and Wildlife Service. Late snow cover at the nesting site affects the numbers of geese that nest and produce young. Those that nest in the arctic regions have a very short span of time in which to build the nest, lay and incubate the eggs, and hatch and raise the goslings in order for the young geese to be sufficiently mature to fly south at migration time. Often the arriving geese must wait before the snow melts sufficiently to allow nesting to begin. If extremely late snow cover delays the geese from finding suitable nesting space, many birds will abandon nesting altogether for that season.

In addition to appropriate nesting habitat, food at the nesting site is important. If late snows have delayed the growth of green grasses the geese need to feed on, they will use stored energy for body maintenance and clutch size will be reduced. If food is in very short supply, the eggs will be reabsorbed into their tissues rather than laid in a nest. Since the homing instinct is very strong in geese, they do not readily move far away to alternate locations for nesting. Instead, the females seem to return to the place where they were hatched to raise their families. When their traditional nesting sites are not available, they may simply skip nesting that season.

Nesting conditions in the northeastern Hudson Bay region, where most of the Atlantic Flyway geese raise their broods, were exceptionally poor in the spring of 1989. The snow was unusually late, covering much of the nesting habitat. Geese have a built-in biological calendar that tells them when it is too late to nest. Eggs must be laid by about mid-June for the young geese to reach sufficient maturity to make the long migration flight to their winter quarters. Dr. Richard Malecki, research biologist with the U.S. Fish and Wildlife Service, visited the Hudson Bay nesting area in July 1989 and found that nesting had been almost a complete failure. Production of Atlantic Canada Geese in the Hudson Bay region has been very low since 1983, but Malecki called 1989 the worst season of the five-year period of decline, according to newspaper ac-

counts.

The other major factor that influences gosling production is the age structure of the population. In populations that include many juvenile birds, the production of goslings in proportion to the size of the total population will be lower due to the smaller number of birds of breeding age. Recent studies have shown that many Canada Geese do not breed before the age of three or even four years. And some birds never breed at all.

Nesting success when the weather is cooperative is high. While nesting outcomes vary with the location, on the average 70 percent of the nests successfully hatch at least one gosling. (Four to six eggs per nest are typical for most species of Canada Geese.) The failure of 30 percent of those nesting efforts can be attributed to three major categories of events. Nest destruction by predators ranks highest as a cause for failure, accounting for about 48 percent of the total loss. Desertion of the nest is another major cause of nest failure at 42 percent. Nests are deserted because the parents are killed or driven off by predators, or because of inhospitable weather such as late freezing or heavy snow. Approximately 9 percent of the nest failure is caused by flooding. Occasionally overcrowding at the nesting site will lead to abandonment of the nest.

The predators differ with the location of the nesting site. In the arctic tundra, the predators include foxes, ravens, jaegers, and herring gulls. In the lower Canadian and U.S. breeding grounds, foxes, coyotes, crows, magpies, and eagles are threats to eggs and goslings. In the Copper River Delta of Alaska, bears have developed a fondness for the eggs of the Dusky Canada Goose.

Counting geese and predicting the numbers of goslings that will be added to the fall flight is not an easy task. Various types of surveys have been used, including observations and counts from the air and on the ground, satellite imagery that indicates snow cover at the nesting sites, and aerial photography. For the past several years, the U.S. Fish and Wildlife Service and the Canadian Wildlife Service have conducted cooperative aerial surveys in the northern nesting areas to assess

Nuisance geese on a suburban lawn.

the conditions for breeding birds. Ron Reynolds from the U.S. Fish and Wildlife Service has made some of these flights over the Arctic. He reports that the flying is often done under less than ideal conditions with late storms, whiteouts, and low temperatures. Data from these flights and other sources are used to predict the fall migration numbers for each of the major Canada goose populations. The estimated fall flight numbers together with other information are used by the four flyway councils in making their recommendations to the Secretary of the Interior on the annual federal hunting guidelines.

NONMIGRATING OR LOCAL GEESE

When spring brings the departure of the migrating ducks and geese, I am always sad to see them leave. I miss their noisy congregations on the river and their calls as they pass overhead. But the spring is a wonderful time to observe and photograph local Canada Geese. When all the migrants have gone, many Canada Geese can still be found throughout much of the United States and the Canadian provinces. Some of these local geese have taken up residence in parks and on golf courses, ponds, and lakes in suburban and even urban locations. Most nonmigrating geese are descendants of birds that were injured and therefore unable to return to their traditional nesting sites. If a pair is reunited following the injury of one of the two, they may eventually nest where they landed. There must be suitable safe nesting habitat for this to occur. Since female geese return to their birthplaces to nest when they reach breeding age, the new goslings do not migrate north. In this way, the numbers of resident geese increase from year to year. Just how many nonmigrating geese there are, no one knows. The Fish and Wildlife Service is beginning to study these birds, especially in the Atlantic Flyway, to try to determine their numbers.

Around Vancouver, British Columbia is a large population of resident geese. Some biologists classify the geese of Vancouver as a separate race of Canada Geese. These birds nest in the great marshes around Vancouver, raise their families there, and then remain in the temperate winter months basking in the warmth brought by the Humboldt Current.

Some flocks of nonmigrating geese have been deliberately introduced to increase goose numbers in places where the population of migratory birds had drastically declined. These geese are descendants of domestically raised geese that were released into the wild. Missouri wildlife managers, for example, transplanted captive Giant Canada Geese to their state and were successful in increasing the flocks there to over 10,000. Rochester, Minnesota; Batavia, Illinois; and several other midwestern cities have nonmigrating Canada Geese of the Giant race living nearby (Swanson 1989). These Giant Canadas trace their lineage back to the captive flocks that were common in the Midwest early in the twentieth century. Farmers discovered that the Giant Canadas were easy to domesticate and that they made superb live decoys for hunting. In Rochester, Minnesota, the municipal power plant provides warm water that keeps a portion of Silver Lake open throughout the cold winter months, enabling the geese to remain in Rochester all year around. The locals are joined by thousands of migrants for the warm water and safety of the town's lake.

NUISANCE GEESE

Much as the local geese may be welcomed and encouraged in some areas, in others they have become a serious nuisance, as have migratory geese who choose urban and suburban locations for their wintering grounds. Since geese like to loaf around fresh water, they may pollute reservoirs and raise the bacteria count in drinking water supplies. They can also destroy lawns, interfere with air traffic, and mess up golf courses and parks. In Stoneham, Massachusetts, for example, during the hot dry summer of 1988, thousands of geese invaded the town in search of green grass to eat. In a newspaper article titled "Town Honked Off at Canadian Gaggle," an Associated Press correspondent reported "Police on horseback have been forced to conduct daily Canada

"Twilight Landing."

geese roundups because of a multiplying gaggle that is stopping traffic, munching parched lawns, and, er, making people more careful where they step. . . . the geese are keeping residents awake at night with their honking."

Chasko and Conover (1988) report that in Connecticut the resident goose population is thriving. They estimate that since the 1950s Connecticut's resident population of geese has risen from 100 to 9,000. That doesn't seem like many geese for such a large state. I know that my relatives in Deep River very much enjoy the geese living in the pond by their home. But it seems that many of the geese have taken a fancy to city life. "We started hearing more and more

complaints from water companies, homeowners, park managers, and golfers. . . . When goose droppings cover a golf course, they add a new dimension to the game," observed Chasko and Conover. The authors surveyed twelve golf course managers from every state east of the Mississippi. From their survey, 42 percent responded that geese were on their courses, and of those, 62 percent felt the geese were a nuisance. Greenwich, Connecticut is a wealthy bedroom suburb of New York City with a problem that money can't solve. The geese have virtually taken over the town's beach area and its parks. People tried electric fences, noise makers, and even shooting blank cannon shots over the heads

of the geese, to no avail. The town had spent a great deal of money cleaning up the pollution that had closed their shellfish beds. Now the geese have polluted the clam beds once more. "I tend to think they're smarter than us," said the manager of the Greenwich parks. "And I think they are winning."

Solving the problems associated with unwanted resident Canada Geese seems nearly impossible to some town authorities. And these problems will only multiply as the resident flocks continue to grow. Perhaps the only answer will be live trapping some of the geese and relocating them to places that want more wild geese like the North and South Carolina refuges.

Mom, dad, and goslings go for a swim.

SUMMER: GOSLINGS ON PARADE

I once asked Claudia Wilds, author of *Finding Birds in the National Capital Area*, if she had any interesting goose tales to share. Her immediate response was no. It seemed that she wasn't especially fond of geese. Then a few minutes later she came back and told me this story, which made it clear why she didn't care for geese. "I remember, soon after I had graduated from college, walking on a nearby golf course with a friend. Suddenly from out of nowhere two Canada Geese came flying straight towards us. It happened so quickly that we both instinctively dropped to the ground. The geese landed on us and began flailing their wings and pulling our hair, making it most difficult to escape. Of course, we had unknowingly strayed too close to their goslings, something I have been careful to avoid since!"

CANADA GEESE, ATTENTIVE PARENTS

From a human perspective, as parents go, Canada Geese must rank among the very best in the world. Both mother and father are totally involved with the care, feeding, and protection of their young. They keep the young goslings within a few feet at all times, not allowing a single gosling to wander off. Canada Geese fiercely defend their goslings against all intruders, even those much larger than themselves, and do not hesitate to attack people, foxes, and dogs.

By contrast, ducks are very different parents, and seem to be very casual about rearing their ducklings. The male duck has nothing at all to do

with the process other than to mate with the female and fertilize the eggs. The mother duck will fend off intruders and try to keep the ducklings close to her, but she is not nearly as committed to defending her brood as the geese are.

As a consequence of this behavior, duckling mortality can be high. They may be nibbled by fish, gobbled by turtles, snatched up by hawks and other birds of prey, or carried off by foxes. Some studies of survival rates for mallard ducklings report losses as high as 50 percent before the ducklings reach maturity. Goslings, on the other hand, usually have a high survival rate. Bellrose mentions studies of mortality rates for hatchlings from birth to flight-age that range from 7 to 28 percent for goslings. Other research points out that in their first year, 10 to 15 percent of young geese may die from predation by foxes, eagles, and other mammals or from disease. In geese, the integrity of the family is tight. On land and on water the goose family moves as a unit. They swim close together, usually mother out front with father behind. Mother and father are constantly on the alert, chasing away large fish and frogs, and of course other ducks and geese. They are also much aware of birds flying overhead.

For several years, I have had the opportunity to observe and photograph the same pair of Canada Geese nesting and raising their family on an island in a suburban pond near my home in Virginia. As I watched this pair over the course of many days, I came to appreciate what mar-

The last gosling to hatch.

"Rearranging the Pile."

A proud goose with her goslings.

velous parents geese are.

During the twenty-eight days that the female goose incubated the eggs, the male remained within a few hundred feet of the nest. Just before hatching, he moved close by and stayed with the female as the goslings hatched. Most bird guides indicate that broods of four to six goslings are common for Canada Geese. My pair of geese have hatched seven and even eight goslings some years. One year, three more goslings mysteriously appeared several days after the hatching, brought apparently by the park personnel for these parents to raise. They seemed to take in the three new goslings without hesitation and raised them with their own seven.

For the first several hours after hatching, mother kept the new goslings tucked in the downy fluff of the nest, sleeping against her. One spring when it was unusually cool, the goose put the goslings under her wing, giving warmth and completely covering them from the elements. Brooding is generally done only the first week

after hatching, although in colder areas it may go on for three weeks until the tiny goslings are able to keep themselves warm.

If the goose does not tuck them against her, the goslings form a pile for sleeping, something they frequently do in the first few weeks of life. The pile appears to function both as a means of keeping warm and as a means of social contact. One of the goslings is always unhappy with its position in the pile, so the pile continually shifts as one or another crawls out from below and tries to climb up top. I have also seen two goslings, three weeks old, lean against each other to slumber.

Several hours after hatching, mother goose rises from her snooze and calls softly to her brood to follow her to the water's edge. She finds the spot with easiest access for the little geese, enters the water, and calls them to her. They obediently plop down into the water, bobbing like little corks, and paddle close behind mother. Their first swim lasts only ten minutes or so be-

Sleepy goslings.

"First Swim."

fore she leads them out to rest. The goslings sleep again before the goose shows them how to feed on the grasses around them. During the first day, they alternately swim, feed, and sleep with both mother and father hovering near them.

During the first three weeks, the goose leads the goslings swimming while the gander follows close behind. Later, either parent may initiate swimming and take the lead position. The little goslings stay close together, often in a line like a gosling parade. If the nest site is far from the safe water necessary for food and rearing the young, the goose may lead the family as much as several miles, sometimes down swift-moving streams (Palmer 1976).

GROWTH OF YOUNG GOSLINGS

When goslings first hatch, they are tiny fluffy balls of yellow and brown fuzz. Their fuzzy down helps them float on top of the water, so they are good swimmers soon after hatching. Goslings are so buoyant during the first two

Mom and her gosling.

weeks that they cannot keep their heads under-water to forage for food in the pond. It is hard to believe that these tiny bits of fluff, small enough to fit into your hand, will be as large as their parents by September. Medium-sized races of Canada goslings weigh from three and a half to seven and a half ounces when they hatch. Eight weeks later they weigh around six pounds (Palmer 1976).

For the first two weeks of their development, the goslings show little change in appearance ex-cept that the bright yellow of their down gradually begins to fade into darker gray brown. The goslings spend much of their time sleeping in the first weeks. They learn to nibble a variety of both land and aquatic plants. Goslings raised in parks very quickly learn that small children often feed them. The goslings run toward children, looking for handouts, while they ignore passing adults.

As the goslings start to lose some of their fluffy down, their wings begin to develop feathers. By the end of their third week, wing feathers and tail

Overleaf: Goose and goslings swimming.

The goslings' first swim, four hours after hatching.

A hungry gosling nibbling on grass.

coverts can be seen. By the end of the fourth week, dark tail feathers and breast feathers are obvious, and the wing feathers have begun to lengthen.

As they grow, the goslings start to copy more of their parents' behaviors. They begin hissing when disturbed after their first week. They also quickly learn the threat postures such as extending the neck and honking. In these early weeks, the young frequently stretch their legs and wings.

About the third week, the goslings are better able to dip for food in the pond. Mother teaches them how to find and eat pond grasses. They have also learned to bathe and stretch and flap their wings by the third week. The family still stays very close together at this time, whether on land or in the water, with mother and father both alert for danger.

By the end of the fourth week, the goslings have lost most of their yellow color, except for their heads, and their tails and wings show definite feathering. In the next two weeks, they stretch and flap their wings vigorously, and undertake their beginning tests of flight. The goslings lift themselves up on their tails to run across the top of the water, flapping their wings, often honking as they go. It is almost as if they are joyfully shouting, "Look what I can do!" They cover seven to ten feet at a time as they dash across the water with these initial preflight trials.

By the thirty-sixth day, the goslings begin to look much more like adults than downy chicks. The white crescent above their tails shows, and the tail feathers and wings are well developed. By the fortieth day, the downy necks have changed from dirty gray to black feathers, and the beginning traces of white cheek patches appear.

The young geese can readily dip below the surface of the water for food, moving their legs to keep their balance underwater as they reach for submerged pond weeds. They frequently feed tail-up at this stage of development.

By the eighth week, the goslings have been

Overleaf: The young goslings learning the aggressive neck-stretching behavior.

Goslings eating pond grass.

Bathing goslings.

"Streeeetch."

transformed into geese. Almost all traces of their baby down are gone, and they are fully feathered. Sometime during the eighth or ninth week, the geese take their first real flight. By this time they have spent much time testing and trying out their wings on land and on water. People raising Canada Geese in captive flocks report that flight is delayed a week or more in these birds, as opposed to those reared in the wild.

While the young are growing, their parents have lost some of their wing feathers in their annual molt. Molting begins for both goose and gander within a few days of each other when the goslings are about two weeks old. During the molt, the parents are unable to fly. Even though flightless, they can run faster than people can and cover long distances if necessary. They generally seek secluded areas at this time, taking the whole brood to some well-hidden location. The entire molt phase lasts five to six weeks. The parents' new wing feathers grow in about the same time or soon after the young are ready to fly. When the whole family is ready for flight, the goose leads them away from the rearing area to feeding and grazing areas. They often go to mud flats and river banks at this time where they can rest and take in grit needed for digestion (Palmer 1976).

Local or nonmigrating geese may remain in the nesting area during the molt. Probably both the limited availability of more secluded areas plus their degree of comfort and safety at the nest site are factors relating to the family's move at this vulnerable time. My geese remained at the nesting pond until all were ready to fly. I was sorry to see them leave, but I knew that the parents would be back the next year to raise another family on the island.

RAISING CANADA GEESE

Some races of Canada Geese can be successfully raised in the farmyard and kept as domestic pets or released into the wild. Especially the Giant Canada Goose is readily tamed and reproduces well in captivity. There are many

"Pre-flight Trials."

documented examples of Giant Goose husbandry early in the twentieth century in the Midwest of the United States and in Canada. They were raised both for food and feathers and as live decoys. Today there are reported to be some 20,000 domesticated large Canada Geese in Ontario and Quebec, raised primarily for food.

Early in the 1900s, a number of farmers in Minnesota and other midwestern states along the major flyways raised Canada Geese. The book *Home Grown Honkers* contains a collection of articles about goose husbandry, most of them detailing how to raise Canada Geese. It also includes some historical accounts of early aviculturists and farmers raising geese. One tells about Martin Gullickson who raised Giant Canadas in Marshall County, Minnesota at the turn of the century. A son related how Martin stole two goose eggs from a nest at Mud Lake and put them under a brooding hen to hatch. From these two goslings his flock grew to thirty large geese that walked freely around the small town and grazed

in the nearby pastures. Some of the birds had clipped wings, but even those that were free to fly away remained in the area. Martin named each goose in the flock. In the fall, he gathered the geese into an old chicken coop and fed them grain; mostly they ate snow for water in the frozen winters. Some years later, the senior Gullickson and a hunting friend were the first in that area to use captive geese as live decoys. This was so successful that other farmers began raising geese for use as live decoys. Soon the culture of Giant Canada Geese developed into a lively business. In 1935, the use of live decoys was outlawed, and so the culture of the Giant Canada Goose dwindled and eventually died out.

Another Minnesotan, Hans Jager, began raising Giant Canada Geese in 1906 quite by accident. He worked in the school system in Owatonna, Minnesota, but he was also a naturalist and aviculturist. He was asked to supply geese for a park in Minneapolis, so he began raising the Canadas. When the goslings were grown and

An adolescent gosling.

These goslings are fully feathered at eight weeks of age.

ready to ship to Minneapolis, he found the director of the park had changed his mind, so Jager continued to care for the flock. He sold a number of the geese to other buyers, including Henry Wallace of Detroit. In 1937, Wallace donated his flock of 332 Giant Canada Geese to Seney National Wildlife Refuge in Michigan. They adapted well to the Michigan refuge and eventually reverted to their former migrational behavior, following the wild birds north to nest in Canada. In 1949, some descendants of these large geese were transferred back to Minnesota to Agassiz National Wildlife Refuge. By then many Giant Canadas had disappeared from Minnesota.

Rochester, Minnesota still had a small number of large Canada Geese, presumed to be Giants, in the 1930s. Dr. Charles and William Mayo built a forty-three-acre lake in 1913 by damming the Zumbro River four miles from town. In 1922, they purchased twenty-two farm-grown geese for their lake, the beginning of a flock that grew each year. In 1926, the state established a wildlife refuge around Rochester, which helped the local flocks to prosper and grow. Silver Lake, a twenty-five-acre lake in the northeastern part of the city, was created in 1936. More geese were purchased to stock this lake. The waters of this lake are warmed by effluent from the municipal power plant built nearby in 1948. Thus, Silver Lake has become a year-round goose haven attracting migrants who join the local flocks for the warm open waters in the dead of winter. Today, Silver Lake may have as many as 10,000 geese during the winter months. Rochester is the farthest north that any flock of wild geese winters in the United States (Swanson 1989).

Of all the subspecies of Canada Geese, the Giant Canada was most often chosen for the breeding flocks, since it was the most adaptable and most easily tamed of all the races. Giants, for example, readily accepted wash tubs and other artificial structures for nesting. In fact, the Giant Canada is reputed to be the easiest of all the species of waterfowl to raise in captivity. They are

"The Goslings Grow Up."

known for their placid temperament and gentle behavior. Other races of Canada Geese being far less adaptable have been much more difficult to raise domestically.

Another race that was recently raised in captivity is the Aleutian Canada Goose. Early in the 1970s when it was determined that the Aleutian Goose was in severe danger of extinction, the U.S. Fish and Wildlife Service brought a few eggs to their research center at Laurel, Maryland. They began raising Aleutian Geese to save the subspecies. By the late 1970s, the Patuxent Research Center was sending 300 young geese annually to the Aleutian Islands in a restocking effort. The size of the flock had grown from 250 to over 5,000 birds by 1982 when the project was completed. The Fish and Wildlife Service considers this to be one of its more successful restocking projects.

Several small breeding farms currently raise waterfowl for zoo collections and for stocking private hunting preserves. In addition to these traditional buyers, a new market for small numbers of captive waterfowl has emerged in the last ten years—the professional waterfowl decoy carver. A number of carvers have established protected ponds where they keep ducks and geese so they may have live subjects close at hand to observe and photograph as models for their carving.

CONSERVATION OF WETLANDS

Summer ripens; the young geese are fledged and flight worthy for the journey south with their families. Will the Canada Geese find abundant wintering grounds in the lower forty-eight? Or will the geese, in their fall migration, discover more of their homelands destroyed by human settlement and agriculture?

Essential to the conservation of Canada Geese is the conservation of goose habitat. And goose habitat is wetlands. Wetlands in the United States have only recently benefited from a developing constituency among citizens determined to preserve them. Marshes were the forgotten wilderness visited by relatively few people. With the notable exception of the Everglades and the Okefenokee Swamp, the watery wilderness areas in the United States have been largely ignored in preservation efforts. Mountains, forests, and hills have received more attention from the public, and as a result, many of the most beautiful and scenic of these places have been preserved as parklands or designated as wilderness areas. After all, parks are for people. People visit and enjoy parks, where they can hike and camp; fish, swim, or boat; or sightsee. Swamps and marshes, on the other hand, are not much fun for people, offering only limited possibilities for recreational use. Fishermen and hunters are the primary visitors to wetlands, and they use these areas only at certain times of the year. Wetlands are for birds, mammals, and fish. To these creatures, the wetlands are home; without wetlands, many of them cannot survive.

Lacking a strong constituency of supporters, wetlands have suffered greatly, largely disappearing in many states. In the United States, we continue to destroy our wetlands at the rate of 300,000 to 500,000 acres per year, according to the National Wildlife Federation's Environmental Quality Index in the spring of 1989. California, for example, has many thousands of acres devoted to magnificent national parks like Yosemite, Kings Canyon, and Sequoia, and to national monuments like Death Valley, Lassen Volcanic, and Joshua Tree. In addition, vast areas are set aside and protected as national and state forests. Glancing at the map of California indicates how much territory these protected lands cover. Nearly one-fourth of the state is protected in parklands and wilderness areas. But what of the vast marshes that once filled the great central valley of California with the musical sounds of huge flocks of ducks and geese? Because the majority of these wetlands were not protected, 92 percent of the marshes in California have disappeared! The marshes have been gobbled up for roads, for farmland, for airports, for garbage dumps. As the wetlands have disappeared, so have most of the wintering waterfowl in the state of California.

The story is much the same in other regions of the country. The prairie potholes in the north central states are almost all plowed under now because no one thought they were valuable enough to preserve. As the potholes have been

Clouds blow over the wetlands.

drained, the production of pintails, redheads, canvasbacks, teals, and ruddy ducks has declined drastically. And Canada Geese have fewer resting places during their migration flights. In the Chesapeake Bay region, much of the fresh water wetlands, as well as the salt marsh habitat, has been destroyed for highways, shopping centers, housing developments, and marinas.

Recognizing the need for conservation of wetlands, several organizations have devoted their time and money to saving these fragile areas. Ducks Unlimited, which celebrated its fiftieth anniversary in 1988, was one of the first major organizations to devote its attention to preserving wetlands. In the half century since the founding of Ducks Unlimited, it has raised nearly one-half billion dollars for conservation. Most of the 550,000 members of Ducks Unlimited are hunters. Other members like me are not hunters but simply concerned people who care about saving ducks and geese and their habitats. Ducks Unlimited Canada, founded in 1937, has 100,000

members. Ducks Unlimited de Mexico joined the other two groups in 1974, adding several thousand more members from Mexico and Central America. Ninety-three percent of the money raised by these three groups goes to conservation projects designed to aid waterfowl. The largest portion of the funds has gone to waterfowl habitat preservation and restoration in Canada where the majority of ducks and geese nest. Approximately 80 percent of the money raised has been used for duck habitat restoration projects in Canada. The Canadian nesting habitat for Canada Geese is largely secure because it is located far to the north beyond the reaches of any development. It is the duck nesting habitat in the Canadian prairies that has been under so much pressure from agricultural interests. Ducks Unlimited funds spent in Canada, therefore, have largely been to support wetland nesting areas for ducks. But in the United States, the wintering habitats for both ducks and geese are severely threatened.

In 1984, Ducks Unlimited decided that the

continuing loss of wetlands within the United States was a cause for great concern. Accordingly, they designated a significant amount of money for the Wetlands America initiative which concentrated on waterfowl-producing states within the United States. Here the organization's money went into matching grants to help the states build and restore wetlands suitable for both ducks and geese. Ducks Unlimited also began a major survey of wetlands on the North American continent using data from a NASA satellite to aid in evaluating the current status of these areas.

When Willie Parker retired from the U.S. Fish and Wildlife Service in 1979, he became actively involved with Ducks Unlimited, often as the guest speaker at fund-raising dinners. As he writes in *Game Warden*, "I am a Ducks Unlimited Life Sponsor and proud of that fact. This international conservation organization offers the only hope for waterfowl. More than eighty percent of the millions of dollars we raise is spent directly to benefit migratory waterfowl in the area where they are most vulnerable, the nesting grounds in the Canadian provinces."

Another organization that early in the 1980s began devoting money to preserving wetlands in the United States is the Nature Conservancy. The Conservancy is a nonprofit conservation organization devoted to "finding, protecting and maintaining the best examples of communities, ecosystems and endangered species in the natural world." In 1984, the Nature Conservancy developed the National Wetlands Conservation Project for which they obtained a $35 million grant from the R.K. Mellon Foundation. Since then, the Conservancy has raised another $86 million in grants from other sources for the wetlands project. This money has been used to buy marshes, desert oases, coastal islands, and prairie potholes. Other Conservancy projects include purchases of portions of the lowlands along the Platte River with habitat critical to the survival of the whooping and sandhill cranes, a small lake and marsh that are the most productive waterfowl breeding spot in Montana, plus numerous small swamps and marshlands throughout the United States. A number of the wetlands projects

"Misty Wetlands."

"Winter Fog."

to which the Nature Conservancy donates funds are joint efforts with Ducks Unlimited and other conservation organizations. The Nature Conservancy has been extremely successful in obtaining cash grants and land donations from corporations, but a significant portion of their funding comes from membership dues.

A recent issue of *The Nature Conservancy News* was devoted to the National Wetlands Conservation Project. I was touched by John Madson's eloquent plea for preserving the last remaining wetlands. A wildlife biologist and author, Madson wrote of his experiences visiting marshes and swamplands across the North American continent.

For me these were good times in a vast variety of wetlands: marshes, swamps, prairie potholes, riverine forests, and that grand flowing river of grass called the Everglades. Days of peace and beauty and sun, as the canoe whispered through worlds teeming with life and spangled with wild iris, calla, lotus, golden spatterdock, and ripening wild rice. Nor have I forgotten those other days of rising wind and lowering sky, with canvasbacks and bluebills coming low and fast out of curtains of sleet—out of the storm's teeth.

Although some lie thousands of miles apart, the wetlands I've seen all have this in common: they are relics of genuine wilderness in otherwise tamed and settled regions. They are the best wild places, as unique and special as any alpine meadow or grove of sequoias.

It has been said that neither wilderness nor innocence can be regained once lost, and that little scraps of native wetlands can never be anything more than trivial souvenirs of a past journey. But a fragment of an original wetland is no less genuine for being only a fragment, and it is anything but trivial—especially when its diversity is compared with the homogeneity of surrounding tamelands. In the world of biology, as in the world of finance, such diversity is our only hedge against unknown and future risks.

Our remaining native wetlands also have this in common: many are in jeopardy, doomed to be drained for crops we do not need, to be filled for resort developments or factories, or simply to be used as garbage dumps. And when the last prairie pothole has been put to wheat, the Achafalaya Swamp made safe for soybeans, and Butte Sink converted to rice fields, a vast part of our wild original wetlands will have been lost forever. It cannot be recalled from computer banks, and no spacecraft can take us where it has gone.

To this I would add only my hope that long after I and my children are gone, others will be able to experience the special moments with the geese that I have been fortunate to share. As I write these closing sentences, it is a clear crisp winter evening after sundown with a deep rosy afterglow lighting the western sky. Suddenly the sky is filled with sound so loud that I hear its melody over the music from my stereo. From across the river, from the corn and wheat fields, the Canadas are winging in low over the tree tops in great waving Vs barely discernible in the deep indigo sky above me. They are settling into the river for their evening's rest. What a glorious sound! What a magnificent sight!—too dark to capture on film, but etched forever in my memory.

Overleaf: Canada Geese flying in the sunset.

WHAT CAN YOU DO TO PROTECT CANADA GEESE?

I urge all who read this book to join me in supporting both Ducks Unlimited and the Nature Conservancy. There are many other fine conservation organizations, but these two in particular spend major portions of their energy and money to preserve our vanishing wetlands, Canada Goose habitat.

Ducks Unlimited
One Waterfowl Way
Long Grove, Illinois 60047

Ducks Unlimited Canada
1190 Waverly Street
Winnipeg, Manitoba R3T 2E2

The Nature Conservancy
1815 North Lynn Street
Arlington, Virginia 22209

Canadian Nature Federation
453 Sussex Drive
Ottawa, Ontario K1N 6Z4

Canadian Wildlife Federation
1673 Carling Avenue
Ottawa, Ontario K2A 3Z1

Canadian Wildlife Service
49 Camelot Drive
Nepean, Ontario K1A 0H3

ABOUT THE AUTHOR

(Photo by Jan Lucie)

Kit Howard Breen combines her artistic interest with her love for wild creatures in *The Canada Goose*, a celebration of the Canada Goose. The book is dedicated to conservationists who share her appreciation for geese and other waterfowl. Kit Breen belongs to several conservation groups including Ducks Unlimited, the Audubon Society, The Nature Conservancy, the National Wildlife Federation, and the Chesapeake Bay Foundation.

The Canada Goose is the third book written and photographed by Kit Breen. Her first book, *Photographing Waterfowl*, is a guide with practical tips for beginning and advanced photography of ducks, geese, and other water birds. The second, *Waterfowl Postcard Collection*, is a gallery of beautiful waterfowl photographs and includes many photographs from the guidebook. Kit Breen's photographs have been published in many calendars including the Audubon Calendar, Wildlife of the West Calendar, Maine Geographic Calendar, and the Waterfowl Calendars from 1983 to 1990, and Fairfax, Birder's World, Country, and Ducks Unlimited magazines.

REFERENCES

Bellrose, Frank C. 1976. *Ducks, Geese and Swans of North America*. Harrisburg, Pennsylvania: Stackpole Books, a Wildlife Management Institute book.

Bellrose, Frank C. 1987. "Goose Migration Corridors." Map in Wesley, David, and Leitch, William. *Fireside Waterfowler*. Harrisburg, Pennsylvania: Stackpole Books.

Bryan, Denver. 1987. "Photo Essay: Cliff Nesting Geese." *Birder's World* (September–October): 22–26.

Cadieux, Charles, L. 1986. *Successful Goose Hunting*. Washington, D.C.: Stone Wall Press, Inc.

Carter, Lloyd. 1988. "What a Mess!" *National Wildlife* (October–November): 42–45.

Chasko, Gregory, and Conover, Michael. 1988. "Too Much of a Good Thing?" *The Living Bird Quarterly* (Spring): 8–13.

Dill, Herbert H., and Lee, Forrest B., editors. 1970. *Home Grown Honkers*. Washington, D.C.: U.S. Department of the Interior, Fish and Wildlife Service.

Hardy, Joel, and Tacha, Thomas. 1989. "Age-Related Recruitment of Canada Geese from the Mississippi Valley Population." *Journal of Wildlife Management* 53(1): 97–98.

Hawkins, Arthur. 1976. "The Role of Hunting Regulations." In Bellrose, Frank C. *Ducks, Geese and Swans of North America*. Harrisburg, Pennsylvania: Stackpole Books.

Hestbeck, Jay, and Malecki, Richard. 1989. "Estimated Survival Rates of Canada Geese Within the Atlantic Flyway." *Journal of Wildlife Management* 53(1): 91–96.

Leopold Aldo. [1966] 1984. *A Sand County Almanac [1949] With Essays on Conservation from Round River [1953]*. Reprint. New York: Random House, Ballentine Books.

Madson, John. 1986/87. "Wetlands." *The Nature Conservancy News* (December–January): 4–7.

Michener, James. 1978. *Chesapeake*. New York: Random House.

National Geographic Society. 1983. *Field Guide of Birds of North America*. Washington, D.C.: The National Geographic Society.

National Wildlife Federation. 1989. "Wildlife." *National Wildlife* (February–March): 34.

Palmer, Ralph. 1976. *Handbook of North American Birds*. Volume 2. New Haven, Connecticut: Yale University Press.

Parker, Willie. 1983. *Game Warden: Chesapeake Assignment*. Centerville, Maryland: Tidewater Publishers.

Peterson, Roger. 1941. *Field Guide to Western Birds*. Boston: Houghton Mifflin.

Rotide, Mike. 1988. "Perfectly Frank." *National Wildlife* (October–November): 24–28.

Scott, Peter. 1980. *Observations of Wildlife*. Ithaca, New York: Cornell University Press.

Steinhart, Peter. 1987. "Empty the Skies." *Audubon* (November): 70–97.

Stokes, Donald. 1979. *A Guide to Bird Behavior*. Boston: Little, Brown and Company.

Swanson, Gustav. 1989. "Photo Essay: Giant Canada Geese." *Birder's World* (June): 28–31.

Terres, John K. 1980. *The Audubon Society Encyclopedia of North American Birds*. New York: Alfred A. Knopf, Inc.

Terres, John K. 1987. "Hitchhikers in the Sky." *National Wildlife* (October–November): 38–41.

Todd, Frank. 1979. *Waterfowl, Ducks, Geese, and Swans of the World*. San Diego, California: Sea World, Inc.

"Town Honked off at Canada Gaggle." 1988. *Bloomington, Illinois Pantagraph*, 25 July.

Williams, Ted. 1989. "Incite: Game Laws Weren't Writ for Fat Cats." *Audubon* (July): 104–113.

U.S. Fish and Wildlife Service. 1984, 1985, 1986, 1987, 1988, 1989. *Status of Waterfowl and Fall Flight Forecasts*. Washington, D.C.: U.S. Department of the Interior.

ACKNOWLEDGMENTS

A number of people contributed to this book. I would like to thank all of them for their help and encouragement. In addition, I owe special thanks to Lloyd Alexander, Frank Bellrose, Larry Hindman, Roland Limpert, and Ron Reynolds for their invaluable information about geese, and to Elizabeth Knight, my editor.

INDEX

"Journey's End."